· MUHLENBERG LIBRARY

D1520646

LANGUAGE AND NATURAL THEOLOGY

JANUA LINGUARUM

STUDIA MEMORIAE
NICOLAI VAN WIJK DEDICATA

edenda curat

C. H. VAN SCHOONEVELD

INDIANA UNIVERSITY

SERIES MINOR

NR. XLVII

1966
MOUTON & CO.
THE HAGUE · PARIS

LANGUAGE AND
NATURAL THEOLOGY

by

BOWMAN L. CLARKE

University of Georgia

201
c597L

1966
MOUTON & CO.
THE HAGUE · PARIS

© Copyright 1966, Mouton & Co., Publishers, The Hague,
The Netherlands.

No part of this book may be translated or reproduced in any form, by print, photoprint, microfilm, or any other means, without written permission from the publishers.

Printed in The Netherlands by Mouton & Co., Printers, The Hague.

To W. D. R.

If the whole of natural theology ... resolves itself into one simple, though somewhat ambiguous, at least undefined, proposition ... a person, seasoned with a just sense of the imperfections of natural reason, will fly to revealed truth with the greatest avidity. ...

D. HUME

We must end with my first love – Symbolic Logic. When in the distant future the subject has expanded ... I suggest that Symbolic Logic ... will become the foundation of aesthetics. From that stage it will proceed to conquer ethics and theology. The circle will then have made its full turn, and we shall be back to the logical attitude of the epoch of St. Thomas Aquinas. It was from St. Thomas that the seventeenth century revolted by the production of its mathematical method, which is the rebirth of logic.

A. N. WHITEHEAD

PREFACE

Contemporary philosophy has forced upon the intellectual world the realization of a basic question – the question of language and meaning. This book is concerned with this basic question as it arises and affects theology, more particularly natural theology and metaphysics. The study is not particularly concerned with evaluating or arguing for any particular religious or metaphysical insights, as such; its primary concern is with the challenge which contemporary philosophy has offered theology and with suggesting a particular approach to the problem of language and natural theology. Few, if any, of the techniques which have been developed by modern semiotics and used here are original. Whatever contribution this study has to offer is limited to the particular way in which it has been suggested that these techniques be applied to what has become one of the more significant philosophical problems of our day. These techniques have been found extremely useful in other areas, particularly the areas of mathematics and the natural sciences. There is no reason to doubt that they can be found equally successful, if used, in the areas of theology and metaphysics. If many of the ideas expressed here appear to be only suggestive and leave the reader with a feeling of incompleteness, then the author can only defend himself with a quote from Russell: "I am sorry that I have to leave so many problems unsolved . . . but the world really is rather puzzling and I cannot help it." [1]

Parts of Chapter I and II were originally published in the *Monist* under the title "Linguistic Analysis and the Philosophy

[1]   B. Russell, "The Philosophy of Logical Atomism", *Readings in Twentieth Century Philosophy*, editors William P. Alston and George Nakhnikian (London, Collier-Macmillan Limited, 1963), p. 348.

of Religion".[2] Two sections of Chapter IV were originally published in *Sophia* as "Proofs for God" and *The Journal of Bible and Religion* as "Language and Revealed Theology".[3] The first three sections of Chapter III were published in *Methodos* as "The Contribution of Logical Positivism". A large part of Chapter V appeared in *The Anglican Theological Review* under the title, "God, Time and Human History". The section in Chapter III on the "Contemporary Outlook" was a paper read to the XIIIth International Congress of Philosophy in Mexico City and entitled, "The Assertive Character of Necessary Statements". I would like to take this opportunity to express my gratitude to the editors of these journals for allowing me to reprint this material and to the publishers who have allowed me to quote material from their copyrighted works.

Also, there are many individuals who deserve an expression of gratitude for their help and encouragement, but it is impossible to list them and thank each individually. At the top of the list should be Charles Hartshorne, who patiently guided the development of some of these ideas in the original form of a dissertation for Emory University; John A. Presto, who helped with proofreading and correcting the manuscript; and Mrs. Sybil Bridges, who spent many hours efficiently typing the manuscript. The list should also include all of my colleagues in the Department of Philosophy and Religion at the University of Georgia; their encouragement and help have been invaluable, as have my years of association with them.

Athens, Ga.   B. L. C.
1965

[2] Copyright © by American Academy of Religion, 1964, and used with permission.
[3] Copyright © by Open Court Publishing Co., 1963, Lasalle, Illinois.

TABLE OF CONTENTS

I

PHILOSOPHY, LANGUAGE, AND RELIGION

To the fifth edition of the *Socratic*, which was devoted to the subject "Contemporary Philosophy and the Christian Faith", the editor appended the following note:

The Oxford University Socratic Club, to which these papers . . . have been read, is an open forum for the discussions between Christians and agnostics of topics relevant to the claim of the Christian Faith to be *true* in some ultimate sense. But nowadays we have to revert to an ancient problem and begin further back – not with truth but with language and meaning. So here we are concerned with 'clarification' rather than with argument. . . . philosophical developments . . . have not only outdated arguments for the existence of God with modern intellectuals, but have thrown doubt on whether sentences mentioning God can ever have any meaning.[1]

This note is significant for this discussion for several reasons. For one thing it introduces one of the earliest public encounters between theology and what has come to be called analytical philosophy. Since these discussions, which were published in 1955, the problem of language and religion has become one of the more lively and interesting problems in philosophical analysis, both in England and America. Most of the works which will be mentioned in this chapter did, in fact, develop from these early discussions in the Socratic Club. This editorial note is also significant for the pointed way in which it states the problem with which this chapter is concerned – that is, the impact which the "revolution in philosophy", as G. Ryle called it, is having on theology and the philosophy of religion. According to the editor ". . . nowadays we have to revert to an ancient problem and begin further back – not with truth but with language and meaning".

[1] *The Socratic*, V (Oxford, Basil Blackwell, 1952).

The historical background of this so-called revolution in philosophy is now well-known. One root lies in England, and, as Ian T. Ramsey suggests,[2] goes back to the turn of the century and owes much to the influence of G. E. Moore and Bertrand Russell. The other lies in Vienna and the now famous Vienna Circle, which evolved in 1923 out of a seminar led by Moritz Schlick. But the man whose influence has been most formative in England and Vienna is Ludwig Wittgenstein. Behind the approach of the Vienna Circle to the problem of language and meaning lay his *Tractatus Logico-Philosophicus*.[3] Likewise the particular style which dominates most British analysis owes more to Wittgenstein's later writings and teaching than it does to either Moore or Russell. And there is no doubt that the unity of aim and method which lies behind this so-called revolution in philosophy, whether in England or on the continent, owes much to the thesis of both the *Tractatus* and his later writings – the thesis that the aim of philosophy is clarification and the method which philosophy uses for this purpose is the method of linguistic analysis.

It was in 1929 that the work of the Vienna Circle became public with the publication of their manifesto: *Wissenschaftliche Weltauffassung – Der Wiener Kreis*. With this manifesto logical positivism was born. The following year saw the inauguration of their periodical, *Erkenntnis*, edited by Reichenback and Carnap. And in this same year logical positivism was first introduced to an international forum of philosophers at the Seventh International Congress of Philosophers at Oxford. At this meeting Schlick read a paper on "The Future of Philosophy". A few quotations from this paper will indicate something of the approach, as well as the enthusiasm and optimism, which characterized this group. Concerning the traditional problems of philosophy he writes,

. . . we see them under a new aspect which provides us with the means

[2] I. T. Ramsey, *Religious Language* (London, SCM Press, Ltd., 1957), p. 4.
[3] Ludwig Wittgenstein, *Tractatus Logico-Philosophicus* (London, Routledge and Kegan Paul, 1922).

of settling all so called philosophical disputes in an absolutely final and ultimate manner. ... it is my firm conviction that we are beginning a new era of philosophy.[4]

This "new aspect" under which philosophical problems are to be seen is expressed by two assertions: (1) philosophy is not a science, and (2) it is the mental activity of clarifying thoughts. To establish the truth of ideas is not the role of philosophy, but the role of the special sciences. Metaphysics, according to Schlick, has been a confusion of these two roles. He writes: "Most of the so-called metaphysical propositions are not propositions at all, but meaningless combinations of words; and the rest are not 'metaphysical' at all, they are simply concealed scientific statements the truth or falsehood of which can be ascertained by the ordinary methods of experience and observation."[5] It was against this background that the now famous, but problematic, verification theory of meaning was proposed.

In England *Erkenntnis* acquired in 1933 a counterpart, insofar as it was concerned with the problem of language and meaning, in the publication of the periodical, *Analysis* – a name which probably testifies as much to the influence of G. E. Moore as to any one other person. It was in 1936, however, that the Vienna Circle and its verification theory of meaning had their formal introduction into England in the form of A. J. Ayer's *Language, Truth and Logic*[6] – a book which Ian T. Ramsey[7] calls a "landmark" in the development of contemporary British empiricism. Two years later an international congress of logical positivists was held in Cambridge.

The peculiar emphases of Vienna, however, were short-lived in England. For by 1955 two prominent members of the British philosophical scene could refer to the original group as "the now

---

[4] Moritz Schlick, "The Future of Philosophy", *Seventh International Congress of Philosophy* (Oxford, 1931), p. 112.
[5] *Ibid.*, p. 115.
[6] A. J. Ayer, *Language, Truth and Logic* (New York, Dover Publications, Inc., n.d.).
[7] Ramsey, p. 12.

defunct Vienna Circle".[8] This period in England between the publication of *Language, Truth and Logic* and Flew and Mac-Intyre's statement has been characterized by Ramsey as the "mellowing" – "the realization that the Verification Principle may be only *one* clue to meaning".[9] Here again one of the dominant influences, along with the groundwork laid by Moore, seems to be Wittgenstein and his movements away from the earlier position of the *Tractatus*. Basil Mitchell contrasts the position of the later British linguistic analysts and their "fresh approach to meaning" with the Vienna Circle's logical positivism in this way:

> ... in place of the dogmatic *assertion* that those statements alone have meaning which are empirically verifiable, they ask the *question* – of any class of statements – 'what is the logic of statements of this kind?' that is to say, 'how are they to be verified, or tested or justified? What is their use and function, what jobs do they do?' [10]

With England's traditional close relationship between philosophy and theology, it would have seemed strange had theology remained unaffected by this philosophical revolution. Yet these new movements in philosophy were slow in being felt in theology. In 1944 John Wisdom published a paper entitled "Gods",[11] which precipitated some discussion of the linguistic problem in its relation to theology. It was, in fact, this paper, according to Flew and MacIntyre,[12] which gave rise to a series of discussions in the Oxford University Socratic Club on theology and language. Still these discussions did not culminate in the publication of the book, *New Essays in Philosophical Theology,* until 1955. This theological lag is indicated by the editors in the "Preface":

> ... it is only in the last few years that attempts have been made to

---

[8]   Antony Flew and Alasdair MacIntyre, editors, *New Essays in Philosophical Theology* (New York, Macmillan, 1955), p. xi.
[9]   Ramsey, p. 13.
[10]   Basil Mitchell, editor, *Faith and Logic* (London, George Allen and Unwin, Ltd., 1957), p. 5.
[11]   First printed in *Proceedings of the Aristotelian Society*, 1944-45, n.s., XLX (London, 1945), pp. 185-206, and reprinted in Antony Flew, editor, *Logic and Language*, First Series (Oxford, Blackwell, 1952).
[12]   Flew and MacIntyre, p. xi.

158635

apply these latest philosophical techniques and insights to theological issues, . . . this is probably the first time that a whole book has been devoted to this enormous job.[13]

In this same year, however, the trend that English theological discussion was beginning to take is indicated by the title of Ian T. Ramsey's inaugural lecture at Oxford: *Miracles – An Exercise in Logical Mapwork.*

Shortly after the Second World War another small group of philosophers and theologians began meeting at Oxford alongside the Socratic Club to discuss informally the current philosophical and theological issues. This group called themselves the "Metaphysicals" – a title which, according to Mitchell, "voiced a common dissatisfaction with the restrictions which tacitly governed philosophical discussion at a time when 'metaphysical' was the rudest word in the philosopher's vocabulary".[14] In 1957 these discussions culminated in the publication of a collection of essays, *Faith and Logic*; their purpose was to meet "a need for careful and sensitive examination of the bearing of contemporary philosophy upon Christian faith".[15] From these early beginnings the problem of religious language has become one of the most discussed problems in philosophy and theology in Britain and America.

No matter what one may think of this basic thesis of Wittgenstein, he cannot ignore the fact that it has changed the vocabulary and style of philosophy in the English speaking countries. I think it could be successfully argued that this revolution in philosophy is, in fact, little more than a change in style and vocabulary and that its aim and method are far closer to the aim and method of traditional philosophy than most would admit. But philosophy, too, has a right to its stylistic fads. It is not the purpose of this discussion, however, to justify this basic thesis or to discuss the virtues or vices of this new style of philosophizing. And there are both. The primary purpose of this discussion is to raise two

[13] *Ibid.*, p. 6.
[14] Mitchell, p. 1.
[15] *Ibid.*, p. 6.

questions: First, if one accepts the thesis that the aim and method
of philosophy is clarification through the analysis of language,
what does this do to that questionable discipline which has traditionally been called the philosophy of religion. And secondly,
how can such a conception of the philosophy of religion meet
the challenge proposed by the editor of the *Socratic* in his closing
sentence: ". . . philosophical developments . . . have not only outdated arguments for the existence of God with modern intellectuals, but have thrown doubt on whether sentences mentioning
God can ever have any meaning".

If the aim of philosophy is taken to be clarification through
the method of linguistic analysis, then it would seem that the
aim and method of philosophy of religion would be the clarification of religious language through an analysis of the language
used in a religious context – that is, language insofar as it is
related to the religious act of worship.[16] This would include the
language of systematic theology, myth, liturgy, sacred writings,
prayers, etc. So interpreted, the philosophy of religion would be
the bridge between the philosophic activity of clarifying and the
religious activity of worship.

In an attempt to clarify what is involved in linguistic analysis,
let me make a few remarks about the nature of language. Plato,
in the *Cratylus* (338 C), was perhaps the first to recognize that
language is an instrument, or tool, associated with a specific art
– the art of communicating and distinguishing. As an instrument,
or tool, it must have a structure adapted to its end – that of
communicating and distinguishing. Aristotle, however, was the
first to clearly express the fact that this structure was reflected
in the rules which, either implicitly or explicitly, govern the use
of the symbols in the language. To speak intelligibly, or meaningfully, is simply to use symbols according to a given set of rules.
Aristotle was also perhaps the first to recognize that there are
different structures and consequently different sets of rules within

---

[16]   A similar conception of the philosophy of religion has been suggested
by Zuurdeeg and Ramsey. See Willem Zuurdeeg, *An Analytical Philosophy
of Religion* (New York, Abingdon Press, 1958) and I. T. Ramsey, *op. cit.*

language. In *On Interpretation,* for example, he writes: "Every sentence has meaning, not as being the natural means by which a physical faculty is realized, but, as we have said, by convention" (17a). In other words, a sentence is meaningful, or intelligible, by virtue of the fact that there are certain rules, or conventions, which govern the symbols which compose the sentence. But he goes on to add: "Yet every sentence is not a proposition; only such are propositions as have in them either truth or falsity. Thus a prayer is a sentence, but is neither true nor false" (17a). And these other sentences, such as prayers, he tells us belong not to science, but to rhetoric or poetry. Thus Aristotle recognizes not only that language is meaningful by virtue of a structure which is reflected in the rules which govern the language, but that there are sub-structures in a language depending upon the end for which the sentences are to be used and the rules which govern this usage.

This idea that meaningfulness is related to the structure of language and the rules which govern its symbols, along with the recognition that there are different sub-languages, or linguistic structures, is one of the more mature insights of the entire analytic movement as it has moved away from the position that verifiability is the sole criterion of meaning. Wittgenstein, for example, in his later work, *Philosophical Investigations,* defines meaning in terms of use: ". . . the meaning of a word", he writes, "is its use in the language".[17] And he finds not one linguistic structure, as he did in the *Tractatus,* but "families of structures more or less related to one another".[18] The story of the criticisms of the original narrowness of the verification principle, its reformulations, and sometimes its outright rejection among the various members and disciples of the original Vienna Circle is likewise well known. Basil Mitchell has expressed this parallel change in British philosophy in this way: ". . . in place of the dogmatic *assertion* that those statements alone have meaning which are

---

[17] Ludwig Wittgenstein, *Philosophical Investigations,* translated by G. E. M. Anscombe (Oxford, Basil Blackwell, 1953), p. 20e.
[18] *Ibid.,* p. 46e.

empirically verifiable, they ask the *question* – of any class of statements – 'what is the logic of statements of this kind?' That is to say, 'how are they to be verified, or tested, or justified? What is their use and function, what jobs do they do?' " [19]

To analyze a language simply means to determine its structure, or the rules which govern the symbols of the language. This includes the purposes for which the symbols are employed by the user, the way in which the symbols refer to or stand for something, the way in which the symbols themselves are related to each other, the rules, if there be any, which govern the truth and falsity of the sentences, etc. Now if the symbols which are used in religious language are meaningful, then they too must have a structure, or structures, which can be analyzed. And just as the analysis of the logical structure of a scientific theory clarifies the nature of the science, as well as the meaning of its symbols, so an analysis of religious language should clarify both the meaning of its symbols and the nature of religion. If, however, philosophy is to make an adequate analysis of religious language, it must not only guard against violating its own integrity, it must likewise guard against destroying the integrity of religious language by forcing upon it alien rules or criteria. The philosophy of religion, in other words, must be an honest attempt to clarify, to discover the rules which do in fact govern the symbols which are used in a religious context. Only in this way will it be a legitimate bridge between the philosophic activity of clarifying and the religious activity of worship. In order to make a little clearer which I mean by an adequate analysis which preserves both the integrity of philosophical analysis and the integrity of religious language, let me illustrate with three concrete cases which I take to be a violation of this integrity.

The first example is a case in which I think an alien rule, or criterion, has been imposed which violates the integrity of religious language. It is the position which R. M. Hare takes in *New Essays in Philosophical Theology*. In a series of discussions en-

[19]   Mitchell, p. 5.

titled "Theology and Falsification", Anthony Flew [20] proposes a criterion for the meaningfulness of assertive statements which might be called the criterion of falsification; that is, a statement which denies nothing, asserts nothing. According to this rule, if the statement 'God exists' asserts something, it must likewise deny something. We must know, in other words, what event or series of events would have to occur in order for us to conclude that the statement 'God exists' is false, otherwise the statement asserts nothing whatsoever. Hare [21] responds to this challenge by maintaining that both the statement 'God exists' and the statement 'God does not exist' are compatible with anything that happens. The difference between these two statements is not a difference between what is *asserted* about the world, but a difference in what he calls a *blick* about the world which, so far as I can determine, simply means a difference in attitudes toward the world.

Although Flew's rule of meaningfulness is questionable on philosophic grounds and will be discussed below, it is Hare's position I wish to examine here, for I think it is questionable on religious grounds. Now Hare himself may use the statement 'God exists' to express his *blick*, or attitude, toward the world. Or he may suggest that we use the statement in this way. This is his privilege. But when the philosopher is analyzing religious language, he must concern himself primarily with how this statement is used in a religious context. No doubt a large part of religious language, and perhaps most of religious language, is used to express attitudes. "Though he slay me, yet will I trust him", for example, is an expression of a worshipful attitude of trust. "O Lord, our Lord, how excellent is they name in all the earth" is an expression of a worshipful attitude of praise. But in both cases God is taken to be the object of trust and praise, not the attitude itself. When we are considering the statement 'God exists' I think we would have to agree with Mascall:

[20] Flew and MacIntyre, p. 98.
[21] *Ibid.*, pp. 99-103.

It is . . . transparently clear to anyone whose judgment is not shackled by a predetermined dogma that, if two men respectively affirm and deny that God exists, they are in fact disagreeing about the nature of reality, and not merely expressing different emotions or aesthetic attitudes.[22]

It may well be that the statement 'God exists' is false or even meaningless, but as it is commonly used it is not, I think, intended to express a person's *blick* or attitude toward the world. And the analytic philosopher who imposes such an alien interpretation on religious statements, even in an effort to salvage them, is violating the integrity of religious language itself.

The second case I want to mention is an example of a position which I would call philosophically inadequate. It is the position of Thomas McPherson in his article, "Religion as the Inexpressible".[23] McPherson accepts the classical positivist's position that religious statements are nonsense, for, according to him, religion *is* the inexpressible. In order to explicate his position he attempts to bring together Rudolph Otto and Wittgenstein. Using Otto's conception of the numinous, McPherson points out that the numinous experience, which he takes to be "the distinctive thing in religion", is precisely that which "cannot be put into words".[24] This he relates to Wittgenstein's statement in the *Tractatus* that "the feeling of the world as a limited whole is the mystical feeling" (6.45). And this, according to Wittgenstein, cannot be said, it "shows itself; it is the mystical" (6.522).

It is not quite clear to me precisely what McPherson means by 'ineffable' here. If he means that religious statements are no more than a series of sounds obeying no rules whatever, then one could not distinguish religious language from the babblings of an idiot – it would be "full of sound and fury, signifying nothing". Obviously this is not what he means. It is clear, however, what Wittgenstein, and perhaps Otto, means by 'ineffable'.

[22]   E. L. Mascall, *Existence and Analogy* (London, Longmans, Green and Company, 1949), p. 94.
[23]   Flew and MacIntyre, pp. 131-143.
[24]   *Ibid.*, p. 137.

Wittgenstein tells us that the ineffable is that which cannot be expressed in the form of propositions, namely, the form itself.[25] And Otto, too, seems to be pointing to the limitations of propositions when he writes: "All language, in so far as it consists of words, purports to convey ideas or concepts – that is what language means – and the more clearly and unequivocally it does so, the better the language." [26] Now if McPherson, like Aristotle, is maintaining that much in religious language cannot be expressed in the form of propositions, then there is no doubt truth in this. But the point which I wish to make is that this still does not relieve the philosopher of religion of the obligation to seek the rules which do in fact govern the different symbols used in religious language.

The metaphor, 'God is a father', for example, does not obey the rules governing propositions, but a metaphor does have a structure and a function of its own. Plato noticed that a metaphor has a structure; it has the structure of a proportion. To illustrate, this metaphor says that 'God is to a man as a father is to his child'. The parodox, "He that loseth his life for my sake shall find it", likewise does not obey the rules for propositions. If it did it would be a contradiction and necessarily false. This does not mean, however, that the paradox cannot have its own meaningful structure and function. The stories related in the Bible may not obey in all respects the rules which govern historical propositions, but they likewise have their own meaningful structure and function. St. Thomas, as well as Dante, recognized that the stories of the Bible have a literal meaning, and in this sense function somewhat as historical propositions, but that the things signified by their literal meaning also have a signification, and it is here that their religious meaning is to be found.

Now any philosophical approach to religious language which retreats into the "ineffable" or into "nonsense" and does not

---

[25] See particularly *Tractatus Logico-Philosophicus*, 4.112-4.115; 5.4711; 6.124; 6.13; and 6.54.

[26] Rudolph Otto, *Idea of the Holy*, translated by J. W. Harvey (London, Oxford University Press, 1926), p. 2.

make an attempt to analyze such meaningful non-propositional structures and their use in religion is simply philosophically inadequate.

The third case which I would consider as an inadequate approach to the problem of religious language is A. G. A. Rainer's [27] response to what has been called J. N. Findlay's ontological disproof of the existence of God. Findlay argues in *New Essays in Philosophical Theology* that the existence of God can only be conceived "in a religiously satisfactory manner, if we also conceive it as something inescapable and necessary, whether for thought or reality".[28] Since necessary propositions, according to him, are senseless, it follows that the proposition 'God exists' asserts nothing. I am not concerned here with the question of Findlay's disproof, which I shall consider below, but with Rainer's response. Rainer answers Findlay by saying that "our assertion of God's existence may be contingent, although God's existence is necessary".[29] He explains in this way: "The 'necessity' of assertions about God's nature and of the connection between his nature and his existence is relative to God's omniscience and not to human reason or experience."[30]

Rainer, unlike our second case, is not maintaining that there are no rules governing the statement 'God exists', rather he is maintaining that we must consider it as obeying God's linguistic rules, not man's. From the point of view of God's omniscience, the statement is necessarily true, but from our point of view it is contingently true. The religious man, however, must in some unknown way, look at the statement from God's point of view. I'm not at all sure what this means. Either God's rules, whatever they may be, are intelligible to us or they are not. If they are, then there is no problem; if they are not, then we cannot even discuss what it means for a statement to be necessary from God's point of view. One thing is certain, and that is that Rainer is in

---

[27] Flew and MacIntyre, pp. 67-71.
[28] *Ibid.*, p. 48.
[29] *Ibid.*, p. 68.
[30] *Ibid.*, p. 68.

danger of placing himself in the position of A. N. Prior's Barthian. In his delightful little dialogue, "Can Religion be Discussed?", Prior has the Barthian say:

> Of course we can only talk nonsense when we try to talk about God
> – our language is the language of sinful men and its utterly unfitted
> for such use. But God, with whom all things are possible, comes to
> our rescue and takes up our words ... and *makes* them carry his
> meaning and his message to men.[31]

Now if religious language, or a part of it, obeys God's rules and
not man's, then apologetics is in trouble, unless the unbeliever
knows God's rules. Or even more puzzling, how do two believers
know they are confessing the same thing unless they can agree
on God's rules? Not only does communication between believer
and non-believer become questionable, but communication between two believers becomes questionable. Perhaps at this point
we should heed St. Paul's advice concerning speaking in unknown
tongues. To retreat into God's omniscience which is hidden from
man or to resort to a miracle for the justification of the meaningfulness of religious language not only makes a philosophical analysis
of religious language impossible, it runs the risk of making religious
language itself impossible. Such a position I would consider inadequate on both religious and philosophic grounds.

If we agree that the meaning of linguistic symbols is linked to
the rules governing their use, then the kind of meaning religious
expressions have depends upon the rules which govern their use
in religious discourse. If religious sentences are used as descriptive sentences – that is, sentences describing or asserting what is
taken to be the case – then they are intended to be descriptive
sentences and must be either true, false or meaningless, that is,
they are intended to be descriptive, but do not conform properly
to the rules governing descriptive discourse. If, on the other
hand, religious sentences are not used descriptively, then they
are meaningful only if there are other rules governing their use,
and the kind of meaning they have will depend upon the kind of

[31]   *Ibid.*, p. 9.

rules governing them. It is the task of the philosopher of religion to discover and make explicit the nature of these rules. This brings us to the second question of this discussion, and the crucial question raised by the editor of the *Socratic*: Can sentences mentioning God ever have any meaning? It will perhaps clarify the nature of this question and the distinction between descriptive sentences and non-descriptive sentences if we consider critically some of the attempts to answer this question in the affirmative.

II

MEANING AND RELIGIOUS LANGUAGE

It is natural to divide the contemporary attempts to deal with the problem of the meaning of religious sentences into those which maintain that all religious assertions are non-descriptive, but meaningful, and those which argue that at least some religious sentences are descriptively meaningful.[1]

A. TWO NON-DESCRIPTIVE THEORIES

One of the earliest attempts to present a non-descriptive theory of religious language was proposed by R. B. Braithwaite. In his Arthur Stanley Eddington Memorial Lecture he divides statements, what I have called descriptive sentences, into three classes: 1) statements about particular matters of fact, 2) scientific statements, and 3) the logically necessary statements of logic and mathematics. He then asks the question: Do religious sentences fall into any of these three classes? His answer is, no. They do not fall into the first class of statements because they are not testable by direct observations. No one takes God to be directly observable. If they fall into the second class, they must be refutable by experience, for according to Braithwaite, "a hypothesis which is consistent with every possible empirical fact is not an empirical one".[2] Braithwaite refuses to assign religious statements

[1] For a summary of these contemporary attempts see W. T. Blackstone, *The Problem of Religious Knowledge* (New York, Prentice-Hall, Inc., 1963). What Blackstone classifies as the "left-wing" and "right-wing" corresponds closely to what I have called "non-descriptive" and "descriptive" theories.
[2] R. B. Braithwaite, *An Empirical View of the Nature of Religious Belief* (Cambridge, University Press, 1955), p. 6.

to this class because religious people do not, as a matter of fact, offer evidence that would falsify religious assertions; rather, he tells us they want to maintain that they are not refutable in any possible world. This, however, is a characteristic of the third class of statements, the logically necessary statements of logic and mathematics. But, Braithwaite argues, the statements forming the third class make no assertions of existence, so religious sentences cannot belong to this class.

If religious sentences do not obey the rules which govern the three classes of descriptive sentences, what kind of rules do they obey? Braithwaite draws an analogy between the use of moral sentences, which likewise do not obey the rules of descriptive sentences, and religious sentences. Moral sentences are used not to describe, but to guide conduct, and in so doing have a "use" and, consequently, are meaningful despite the fact that they are non-descriptive. His thesis is that religious sentences, like moral sentences, are used primarily to guide conduct; they too are non-descriptive, but meaningful. The primary use of a moral assertion is to express the intention of the asserter to act in a particular sort of way, specified in the assertion – to subscribe to a policy of action. Religious sentences, according to Braithwaite, are likewise used to express the believer's intention to follow a specified policy of behavior. Religious expressions are, in a sense, veiled moral sentences; but unlike moral sentences, which are clear and straightforward, they are tied together into a whole system, veiled in metaphor, story and myth for psychological reasons and include the behavior of the inner life as well as external behavior. He tells us, for example, that "to assert the whole set of assertions of the Christian religion is both to tell the Christian doctrinal story and to confess allegiance to the Christian way of life".[3]

Another similar view, and one which will, I think, make both the virtues and vices of Braithwaite's position clearer, is Willem Zuurdeeg's theory of convictional language. Zuurdeeg distin-

[3]   *Ibid.*, p. 24.

guishes between "use-language", which seems to correspond to Braithwaite's three classes of statements, and "is-language", which he calls convictional language: "We *use* a scientific terminology, we *are* our convictions." [4] Sentences of the latter kind, convictional language, have generally been considered as non-cognitive and termed: "emotive", "volitional", or "appeal" sentences. But such terms, our author argues, are insufficient to express, for example, the communist's dedication to his cause or the Moslem's loyalty to Allah. According to him, emotions, will and persuasive intention come into play, but likewise does intellect and other aspects of the personality: the "whole person is involved". [5] Under convictional language Zuurdeeg includes all persuasions concerning the meaning of life, good and bad, gods and devils, the ideal state or society, the meaning of history, of nature, and "the All".

The nature of convictional language, as Zuurdeeg views it, may be made clearer by considering his contrast between it and indicative language which seems to correspond to Braithwaite's first two classes of statements. [6] He is careful to point out that to contrast convictional language with indicative language is not to imply that convictional language "is arbitrary, outside the range of intelligent discussion". [7] Nor does it mean "that indicative language refers to reality, whereas convictional language is a matter of fancy or imagination. Both convictional and indicative languages refer to 'reality' ". [8] Yet, he adds, "the 'reality' meant

---

[4] Willem Zuurdeeg, *An Analytical Philosophy of Religion*, p. 57.

[5] *Ibid.*, p. 2.

[6] What I have called descriptive language, Zuurdeeg classifies as: 1) Indicative, which is concerned with "description, comparison and explanation" and includes both everyday language and the purified language of science; 2) Analytical language, the language used by philosophers to talk about meanings and 3) Tautological language, which is the language of logic and mathematics (*ibid.*, p. 44). Braithwaite places indicative and analytical language in classes one and two (see Braithwaite, p. 11) and tautological language corresponds to Braithwaite's third class.

[7] Zuurdeeg, p. 45.

[8] *Ibid.*, p. 45.

is not the same in both cases".[9] The modern scientist, he tells us, no longer claims that his language refers to the "real" nature of the universe. He uses his theories as hypotheses to explain certain phenomena, to describe facts and to predict future events. Scientific theories "do not reveal anything to us about the 'real nature' of 'reality' ".[10] Yet our author adds: "still these theories have reality in mind, or better, a certain aspect of reality".[11] What Zuurdeeg seems to be saying in these passages is that when a scientist, for example, uses indicative language, he abstracts from "reality" certain phenomenal aspects for his own scientific purposes, while the man who uses convictional language claims to speak about "the totality of reality as he sees it in the light of his specific convictions".[12] Convictional language, then, expresses a *Weltanschauung*. But, our author warns us, this is not to be taken as a passive viewing of the world. Rather, it is all our convictions, integrated more or less into a coherent whole, which form the basis of our actions, and, consequently, make us what we are. The man who speaks convictionally *is* his word.

In both of these positions there is a clear insistence upon the fact that religion involves some specified policy of behavior or a way of life. For Braithwaite religion includes a specified type of behavior of the inner life as well as external moral behavior, and Zuurdeeg underscores this by saying, "we *are* our convictions".[13] If this is true, and certainly few would deny it, then it should follow that any given analysis of religious language must relate religious sentences to specified types of human behavior. It is, however, at the point of what it is religious sentences are about that we find what appears to be a sharp disagreement. Braithwaite, for example, tells us that religious sentences are *about* our *intentions* to follow a specified policy of behavior; whereas, according to Zuurdeeg they are about "life", "actions (good and bad)", "gods

[9]   *Ibid.*, p. 45.
[10] *Ibid.*, p. 45.
[11] *Ibid.*, p. 45.
[12] *Ibid.*, p. 46.
[13] *Ibid.*, p. 57.

and devils", "ideal states and societies", "history", and "nature", "the All", "reality". It seems to be his thesis that convictional language states what we believe to be, or are convicted is the case concerning these, and that we act or behave in certain ways depending upon what we believe to be the case concerning these things.

Whatever the nature of moral sentences, religious language does include many moral sentences. This is not in dispute. The question raised by this contrast between Braithwaite and Zuurdeeg is this: Can all religious sentences be taken as sentences about the believer's intention to follow a specified policy of behavior including both his inner and outward behavior? Or must at least some religious sentences be taken as asserting something about some entity – that such and such is the case? Suppose, for example, we have two believers A and B, and A utters the sentence, 'God loves all men', and B rejoins, 'God does not love all men'. Are A and B merely confessing an intention to behave differently or does their believing the utterances to be true, that is, describe what is the case, result in different behavior? Of course, Braithwaite accepts the first alternative. I feel confident, however, that most religious people would choose the second alternative. Why has Braithwaite chosen the first? Certainly it is not because he thinks that religious people would chose the first alternative. He has chosen the first because had he chosen the second alternative some sentences about God would have to be taken as descriptive, or as statements. In fact, the plausibility of his position rests upon three things: 1) the assumption that his three classes of statements are exhaustive, 2) the rejection of religious sentences from all three classes, and 3) the confusion of the logical interpretant of a sign with the object of that sign. The first two lie behind most contemporary discussions in philosophy and, particularly, contemporary discussions of religious language. But both of these points need to be carefully and seriously examined in any adequate discussion of religious language. For if, as I think most would agree, at least some religious sentences have been traditionally taken as descriptive, then to deny the possibility becomes a rather crucial issue. Thus, the first task in any adequate theory of religious language must be to examine religious discourse and the rules of descriptive discourse and see if Braithwaite's rejection of the second alternative is justified.

The third point upon which Braithwaite's theory rests, the confusion of the logical interpretant of a sign with the object of that sign, lends an air of plausibility to the first alternative in the light of Braithwaite's rejection of the second. And here I have in mind the distinction between the logical interpretant and the object of a sign made by Peirce,[14] a man who has unfortunately been too long overlooked by philosophers interested in linguistic analysis. Take, for example, as a sign the statement, 'That is a chair'. The object of the sign is that entity which the sentence is about, that entity which is taken to be a chair. The logical interpretant of the sign is that pattern of behavior which we exemplify when we believe an entity to be a chair, or accept the sentence, 'That is a chair', as true. Now a pattern of behavior which we exemplify under certain conditions, a logical interpretant, is quite different from the entity, the object of the sign, which illicits this behavior. Likewise, God, the object of religious faith and the object of at least some religious sentences, may illicit different patterns of behavior, but this need not mean that different confessions about God are no more than different confessions about our intentions to behave in different ways. Of course, it is quite easy to specify uniquely an entity such as the one taken to be a chair; we can do it merely by pointing and uttering the word, 'that'. Consequently, it is quite easy in a case such as this to distinguish between the object and the logical interpretant. But it is another matter to specify uniquely an entity named God which is the object of the sign, 'God loves all men'. And it is this difficulty which makes the confusion of the logical

---

[14] See particularly C. S. Peirce, *Collected Papers*, edited by Charles Hartshorne and Paul Weiss (Cambridge, Harvard University Press, 1931-35), V, 464-8 and 470-90. (The numbers cited in *Collected Papers* refer to paragraphs.)

interpretant of this sign with the object of this sign possible. If, however, one is to take seriously the thesis that religious language contains descriptive sentences about God, then he must be able to specify uniquely an entity which is the object of those sentences. An investigation of this possibility is the second major task of a theory of religious language.

It may appear somewhat paradoxical that I have used Zuurdeeg's theory of convictional language as a contrast to Braithwaite's theory of religious language in order to clarify and criticize the non-descriptive character of Braithwaite's theory and have, at the same time, classified Zuurdeeg's own theory as nondescriptive. This paradox, however, arises from what I take to be an unresolved dilemma in Zuurdeeg's own theory. Like Braithwaite he begins by rejecting religious sentences from the class of sentences generally considered as descriptive. Although Zuurdeeg is not too clear on this point, his reasons seem, in general, to be three: 1) Indicative language is only about a certain aspect of "reality", while convictional language concerns the "totality of reality". 2) Convictional language is "related to matters of ultimate importance", while indicative language "implies an element of distance, of reflection".[15] 3) There are no methods for obtaining the truth or falsity of convictional sentences. He denies, for example, that convictional language contains indicative elements because "there are neither scientific nor philosophical proofs or arguments which can validate or invalidate any conviction. There is no public, objective court of reason which can decide who is wrong and who is right." [16]

The first reason seems to give no adequate justification for excluding religious sentences from the class of indicative sentences, unless for some reason it is impossible to speak descriptively about the "totality of reality". The second of these reasons seems to be based upon a strange dichotomy between the ability to hold an important belief and the ability to reflect upon its

[15]   Zuurdeeg, p. 59.
[16]   *Ibid.*, p. 56.

truth or falsity. Even if this dichotomy exists it is not a linguistic or logical distinction but a psychological fact which may pose a practical problem. On the other hand, in proposing this distinction Zuurdeeg may be maintaining that convictional language is "related to matters of ultimate importance" in that it is evaluative and that evaluative sentences are neither true nor false; consequently, there is no possibility for reflecting upon their truth or falsity. In fact, he seems to be maintaining this when he tells us that Biblical theology "cannot be proved or disproved, either by logical reasoning or by empirical evidence. It is an appraisal, an evaluation." [17] If this is the case, then we are led to the third reason given for the non-descriptive character of religious language; that is, there is no method for determining the truth or falsity of convictional sentences. But here there seems to be a confusion between the ability to determine the truth value of a sentence by certain specified methods, logical and empirical evidence, and the ability to give truth conditions for a sentence. If truth conditions can be given for a sentence then the sentence should qualify as a descriptive sentence, even though we may not be able to determine whether or not the conditions do in fact hold. Here again Peirce may be of help. To hold a belief, according to Peirce, is to accept a sentence as true; that is, to be willing to act as if the truth conditions did in fact hold.[18] Now there may be many methods whereby we come to hold a belief, or to accept a sentence as true, but this is a different problem from truth conditions. We may accept it on the basis of authority, because it is pleasant, on the basis of the rules of logic, or on the basis of that amorphous thing called the scientific method. But the question of which method is not the question as to whether or not the sentence is descriptive. The question of method

---

[17] *Ibid.*, p. 291.
[18] I have taken the liberty of rephrasing Peirce in more contemporary terminology. He uses such terminology as: "Belief ... puts us into such a condition that we shall behave in some certain way, when the occasion arises." "We think each of our beliefs to be true, and, indeed, it is a mere tautology to say so." See Peirce, V, pp. 358-87.

is the question of what is the best way, to use Peirce's term, of fixing belief; that is, which method is most likely to determine whether or not the truth conditions do in fact hold.

Neither the strength of conviction, nor the importance of the belief to the believer, nor the method whereby the believer fixes his belief has anything to do with the descriptive character of the language which is used to express the belief. Two men, A and B, for example, may equally well accept the same sentence as true, that is, be willing to act as though the truth conditions did in fact hold. Yet, A may hold his belief with great conviction, whereas B may hold his weakly; A's belief may be quite important to him, whereas B's belief may be trivial to him; A may have accepted his belief on the basis of authority, whereas B may have come to accept his belief on the basis of a long and patient observation of a set of facts. If the truth conditions of the sentence were the same and if the two men acted as though these conditions did in fact hold, why would anyone want to say that the sentence in the case of A is convictional and non-descriptive, whereas in the case of B the same sentence is indicative and descriptive?

If Zuurdeeg, on the other hand, wishes to maintain that truth conditions cannot be given for convictional sentences, then clearly no one would classify his theory as descriptive and he would have a clear linguistic distinction between convictional and indicative language. If he does maintain this, that convictional sentences are purely "appraisals, an evaluation" and have no truth conditions, then one is hard pressed to find a distinction between his theory and Braithwaite's theory. Can convictional sentences be any more than expressions of the believer's intention to behave in a certain way? But whatever position Zuurdeeg would take as to the character of evaluative sentences, or appraisals, he is still faced with a serious problem: Does it make sense to say that we can make meaningful evaluative sentences about God, if, at the same time, we can make no descriptive sentences about him? I can, for example, utter the sentence, 'My mother is more valuable than my dog', but how could that sentence be meaningful under any theory of evaluative sentences unless I could also make descriptive sentences about my mother and my dog? If it were impossible to make descriptive sentences about my mother and my dog, how would anybody, including myself, know what was being evaluated? I can see how one might make meaningful evaluative sentences about life, actions, states and societies, history, and nature, for we can likewise make descriptive sentences about them; but I do not see how one can make even evaluative sentences about gods and devils and "the all", if we cannot make, as Zuurdeeg seems to maintain,[19] any indicative, or descriptive, sentences about them. How would anyone know what was being evaluated or appraised?

B. TWO DESCRIPTIVE THEORIES

It is precisely the attempt to give some descriptive meaning to the word, 'God', that forms the major burden of Ian T. Ramsey's task in *Religious Language: An Empirical Placing of Theological Phrases*. Ramsey places himself in the "third stage" of the development of recent thought – the "mellowing" which "came with the realization that the Verification Principle may be only *one* clue to meaning, so that propositions, however odd by verificationist test, may yet have a meaning of their own".[20] Religious language, for Ramsey, is one logical map with its own "schematism", its own logical differences, and its own brand of "facts", and which has a place in the possible "one comprehensive language map".[21] In investigating the distinctive logic of religious language, Ramsey tells us that we must ask two questions: 1) To what kind of situation does religion appeal? Or, what kind of

---

[19]   Zuurdeeg, p. 130.
[20]   Ramsey, p. 13.
[21]   I. T. Ramsey, *Miracles – An Exercise in Logical Mapwork* (Oxford, Clarendon Press, 1952), p. 3.

empirical anchorage have theological words? 2) For these situations, what kind of language is appropriate?

In answering the first question, Ramsey proposes that the religious situation is a discernment-commitment situation in which there is an "odd discernment" and a "total commitment". He illustrates what he means by "odd-discernment" by suggesting parallel situations in ordinary experience, situations which we say "come alive", in which the "light dawns", the "ice breaks", or the "penny drops". Ramsey admits that the words used in such situations tell us very little in a straightforward manner. But they are not meant to. They may be compared, he tells us, to mathematical operators which themselves "mean' nothing", but are "directions of procedure if we want to discover what the mathematical writer has in store for us".[22] Thus, the function of these words is primarily to direct us to a kind of situation which cannot be described in straightforward indicative language.

It is a response involving our whole personality that forms the second element in the religious discernment-commitment situation – total commitment. Ramsey finds parallels in the loyalty which some have towards a school, a college or a nation, or even the commitment to certain axioms of mathematics. In fact, religious commitment, according to Ramsey, is like the former parallels in being "personal", and is like mathematical commitment in being "universal": "It combines the total commitment to a pastime, to a ship, to a person with the breadth of mathematical commitment." [23] Here he seems to have reference to the universal applicability of mathematics, for he adds: in this way it is "a commitment suited to the whole job of living".[24]

Given this characterization of the religious situation in terms of an odd discernment, uniquely personal in nature, and a total commitment which is both personal and universal, that is, applicable to all of life, we have our empirical anchorage for reli-

---

[22]   Ramsey, *Religious Language*, p. 23.
[23]   *Ibid.*, pp. 35-36.
[24]   *Ibid.*, p. 36.

gious phrases. We must now turn to the second question: What kind of language is appropriate currency for such a situation. This type of situation, Ramsey tells us, suggests that religious language will be logically odd in at least two ways: First, if religious language, as the first element, odd discernment, suggests, deals with situations which are "perceptual with a difference, perceptual and more", then we would expect its language to be "an object language and more, i.e. object language which has been given very special qualifications, object language which exhibits logical peculiarities, logical impropriety".[25] These logical improprieties will be similar to the logic of nicknames. Here "the 'object' reference is at a minimum"; their purpose is "to evoke a distinctly personal situation".[26]

Secondly, the examples paralleling the second element in the religious situation suggest that we may expect religious language to contain siginificant tautologies, "tautologies whose function is to commend those key words – those ultimates of explanation – which ... arise in connection with ... its character as commitment".[27] These ultimate key words, or tautologies, as Ramsey prefers to call them, are parallel to the axioms of mathematics which are reached "when questions have pushed us to the 'irreducible points' of a particular system", and which "express in tautologies, in necessary propositions, the loyalty, the option of the mathematician, as he posits the particular conventions".[28] Take, for example, the word, 'God'. For a religious man 'God' is a key word; it is "an irreducible posit, an ultimate of explanation expressive of a kind of commitment he professes".[29] However, God must be "talked about in terms of the object-language over which it presides, but only when this object-language is qualified".[30] Once qualified, then it becomes currency "for that

---

[25]   *Ibid.*, p. 38.
[26]   *Ibid.*, pp. 38-39
[27]   *Ibid.*, p. 40.
[28]   *Ibid.*, p. 45.
[29]   *Ibid.*, p. 47.
[30]   *Ibid.*, p. 47.

odd-*discernment* with which religious *commitment* . . . will necessarily be associated".[31] No religious apologetic, teaching, or theology which does not evoke the appropriate kind of situation, its empirical anchorage, and recommend language of suitable currency can be considered adequate or worthwhile.

Given Ramsey's characterization of the religious situation and his notion of the word 'God' as a key word, or tautology, let us see how "object-language with its appropriate qualifications" is used in order to talk about God and his attributes and to evoke the religious situation. First, let us examine two traditional attributes of negative theology, immutability and impassibility, and see what Ramsey considers to be their "logical behavior". He points out that two characteristic features of all perceptual situations are change and interaction which change seems to presuppose. "The attributes of negative theology", according to him,

. . . fix on such characteristics of perceptual situations, and whisper in our ears in contrasting denial: Change? Yes, but there's something which does not change, which is 'immutable'. . . . or, confronted with interaction, the whisper now is 'impassible' . . . interaction is not the whole story.[32]

These attributes, impassibility and immutability, invite us to observe the changing interacting world until the "penny drops" and we have a discernment, a "sense of the unseen", and "apprehend something which remains invariable in the situation despite what is so visibly changing".[33] Thus, two words, 'passible' and 'mutable', are taken from our object language, qualified with the negative prefix, 'im', and become currency for evoking the religious situation and for talking about that which is "discerned" and demands our "total commitment".

Another method of qualification which Ramsey proposes is the method of "model and qualifier". This method gives us such attributes as *First* Cause, *Infinitely* Wise, *Infinitely* Good, Crea-

[31]   *Ibid.*, p. 47.
[32]   *Ibid.*, p. 50.
[33]   *Ibid.*, p. 51.

tion *ex nihilo*, and *Eternal* Purpose. Each of these phrases has in it a model, cause, wise, good, creation and purpose, which is taken from the object language and which comes from our ordinary experience and "founds the theological story on empirical fact".[34] But each word has a qualifier (in italics) which prescribes a special way of developing each story until a typical religious situation is evoked. For example, in the phrase 'First Cause', the model, 'cause', specifies a particular situation in ordinary experience and gives us a straightforward picture. However, the qualifier, 'First', is a directive for us to continue moving backward. And this directive to move backward and still backward is always able to be obeyed until the "light dawns" and we have a "sense of the unseen"; a different situation is evoked.

In all these illustrations, it is in relation to this different situation that is evoked, the religious situation, that the word God is posited. And it is the ability of these qualified object words to evoke this different situation that makes them currency for talking about God. Although the word God and the words for his attributes have this empirical anchorage, they have a different logical status from the words in our object language. As a mathematical parallel, Ramsey [35] suggests a succession of sums as 1; 1 and $\frac{1}{2}$; 1 and $\frac{1}{2}$ and $\frac{1}{2^2}$; 1 and $\frac{1}{2}$ and $\frac{1}{2^2}$ and $\frac{1}{2^3}$; ... 1 and $\frac{1}{2}$ and $\frac{1}{2^2}$ ... $\frac{1}{2^{n-1}}$. As this series of sums proceeds, at some point the "penny drops" and 2 comes to mind. Yet, 2 is a number outside the series of "a different logical status altogether from the terms of the series, but a number which might be said to preside over and label the whole sequence of ever expanding sums".[36]

What can be said for Ramsey's attempt to give "empirical", or descriptive meaning to the term, 'God?' Unfortunately, his analogies and metaphors sometimes tend to obscure more than they reveal. In comparing religious phrases to nicknames, he tells us that the "object" reference is at a minimum; the primary

---

[34] *Ibid.*, p. 6.
[35] *Ibid.*, p. 69.
[36] *Ibid.*, p. 70.

purpose of religious phrases is to "evoke". This is taken to mean, for example, that in using a word such as 'immutable', the reference to objects is at a minimum, rather the word is used primarily to evoke the odd-discernment-total-commitment situation. This word "evokes" by directing us to perform an action: we are told to fix our attention on the changing character of perceptual situations until they "whisper in our ears" a contrasting denial: "Change? Yes, but there's something which does not change." Ramsey seems to be suggesting that the traditional terms used for the attributes of God, and consequently to describe him, are now to be used as "directions of procedure" if we wish to "discover" God.[37] Surely Ramsey does not mean that these terms are used to evoke an encounter, or an immediate intuition, of God himself. This would be a rather strange theory as well as contrary to the actual use of these terms in the history of philosophy and religion. If, however, one remembers the British empirical tradition and the problem of the origin of our ideas, one can immediately see a similarity between Ramsey's use of models and quantifiers and the procedures of the empiricists for treating the origin of ideas like infinity. Is Ramsey, then, giving us a procedure for discovering the origin of the idea of God? Some of his language, particularly his first question, "What kind of empirical anchorage have theological words", seems to suggest this. Here I must confess that I feel something of the confusion of Gilson after reading William James: "I still want to know if my religious experience is an experience of God, or an experience of myself."[38] Is it an experience of God which is evoked by these terms, or is it the idea of God that is evoked? In the case of 'immutability' surely Ramsey is suggesting no more than the way in which the idea of God originates from our experience of perceptual change. But what of the question of the existence of a unique individual which is immutable, impassible, a first cause,

---

[37] See Ramsey's reference to the mathematician's use of terms, *Ibid.*, p. 23.
[38] Etienne Gilson, *Reason and Revelation in the Middle Ages* (New York, Charles Scribner's Sons, 1938), p. 97.

infinitely wise, etc.? Certainly this is a crucial question for religious language. The attitude of worship, which Ramsey calls the "one 'factual' reference",[39] assumes that there is an individual which possesses these attributes, and Findlay is quite right: "all attitudes presume characters in their objects, and are, in consequence, strengthened by the discovery that their objects have these characters, as they are weakened by the discovery that they really haven't got them".[40] The crucial problem is: Does the sentence, 'There is a God', have descriptive meaning? It is not sufficient simply to show that we have an idea of God. Worship assumes the fact of the existence of God, not merely the fact of the idea of God. Thus we are forced to raise the question of the truth conditions of the sentence, 'There is a God', a question which Ramsey has not faced.

John Hick is one of the few writers who have attempted to work out a descriptive theory of religious language and faced the problem of truth conditions. Hick begins by characterizing what he calls a "total commitment" – "an individual's *en bloc* interpretation of his entire past and present experience in all its aspects".[41] Here we are concerned with the character of the universe as a whole. As illustrations of such a total interpretation, he proposes theism and naturalism. Neither of these total interpretations, says Hick, can be more probable than the other since each concerns the totality. "Nothing", he argues, "can be said to be probable *per se* but only in relation to data beyond itself".[42] Consequently, since there are no data available beyond the totality called the universe, one total interpretation is as probable as another, given all data in this life. Beyond the principle of non-contradiction, there is no means in this life whereby a total interpretation may be considered falsified: "There is no test observation, no crucial instance such that if A occurs theism is

---

[39]   Ramsey, *Religious Language*, p. 185.
[40]   Flew and MacIntyre, p. 50.
[41]   John Hick, *Faith and Knowledge* (Ithaca, Cornell University Press, 1961), p. 134.
[42]   *Ibid.*, p. 135.

shown to be true, while if B occurs theism is shown to be false." [43] In other words, truth conditions for a total interpretation cannot be formulated with reference to the data of this life. Does this, then, make the sentence, 'There is a God', non-descriptive? No, argues Hick; for truth conditions can be formulated with reference, not to this life, but to the afterlife. Thus, he proposes the principle of eschatological verification as a means for assuring that there are truth conditions for the theistic total interpretation. The truth conditions are formulated, not in terms of this world, but the next.

There is no doubt that Hick's theory is ingenious and is probably a sophisticated formulation of what many religious laymen, not versed in the intricacies of theology and modern philosophy, would doubtless say. And for this reason it does have much to recommend it. Despite this, however, there are two serious difficulties in Hick's theory. One concerns the eschatological nature of the truth conditions for theological statements and the other concerns the status of the sentence, 'There is a God'. The first of these difficulties has been pointed out by William Blackstone. Blackstone points to the fact that Hick assumes the descriptive nature of several religious terms, such as the afterlife and the Kingdom of God, in order to formulate the truth conditions of other religious sentences. "This is", writes Blackstone, "obviously a question begging technique, for the assertion-status, or factual meaningfulness, of all these religious claims is under question by the philosophical analyst".[44] Unless Hick can give descriptive meaning to the term, 'afterlife', the principle of eschatological verification itself is meaningless.

The second difficulty concerns the logical status of the sentence, 'There is a God'. Even if it were possible that one could give a descriptively meaningful interpretant for the term, 'afterlife', and could, as Hick wishes, formulate truth conditions for the sentence, the sentence would be a contingent statement, and

---

[43] *Ibid.*, p. 145.
[44] Blackstone, p. 114.

the existence of God, a contingent fact. Since these truth conditions are such that they may be found to hold or they may not
be found to hold, this means that God may exist or he may not
have existed. In fact, according to this theory, the world could
have existed and God at the same time not have existed. This
does violence to one of the key notions in the concept of God –
that of creator. If it means anything it means that the world could
not have existed without him. Theologians have generally interpreted this religious notion of a creator in terms of necessary
existence, a problem we must now face.

C. FINDLAY'S ONTOLOGICAL DISPROOF

J. N. Findlay in his essay, "Can God's Existence be Disproved?",
has done an excellent job of clarifying precisely what is involved
in the sentence, 'There is a God'. He begins by characterizing
the religious attitude as one in which we tend "to abuse ourselves before some object, to defer to it wholly, to devote ourselves to it with unquestioning enthusiasm, to bend the knee
before it, whether literally or metaphorically".[45] This is simply
to take the first great commandment as a characterization of the
religious attitude: "Thou shalt love the Lord thy God with all
thy heart, and with all thy soul, and with all thy mind, and with
all thy strength" (Mark 12 : 30). Now Findlay raises this question: What would be an adequate object of this religious attitude?
What kind of being could evoke or justify such an attitude? It
cannot be, he argues, a being which merely *happens* to exist, nor
one on which other objects merely *happen* to depend. It must be
a thing upon whom everything that exists and everything that is
of value ultimately depends. Thus, "not only must the existence
of other things be unthinkable without him", he writes, but "his
own non-existence must be wholly unthinkable in any circumstances. . . . There must, in short, be no conceivable alternative

---

[45]   Flew and MacIntyre, p. 49.

to an existence properly termed 'divine' ".[46] Another being, as he says, might deserve the veneration cannonically accorded to the saints, but not the worship we properly owe to God.

In a very subtle way, Findlay has brought together the essence of the ontological argument and the argument from contingency to give us an explication for the only adequate object of the religious attitude expressed in the first great commandment. In explicating the term 'God' in this way, he has also clarified the logical status of the sentence, 'There is a God'. Since "the existence of other things is unthinkable without him", then by the definition of God, the sentence 'There is a God' must be a necessary condition for any contingent sentence. This is the essence of the argument from contingency; that is, the existence of any contingent being is dependent upon the existence of God. The other phrase, "his own non-existence must be wholly unthinkable in any circumstances", gives the essence of the ontological argument; that is, the negation of the sentence 'There is a God' results in a contradiction. Thus, Findlay concludes that if the word 'God' is used to refer to a being who is an adequate object of religious worship, then the sentence 'There is a God' cannot be verified or falsified by any contingent state of affairs whatsoever. It follows, then, that if the concept of God is not a self-contradiction, such as 'round square', the sentence must be logically or necessarily true.

But what, then, is Findlay's disproof? He writes: "Plainly (for all who share a contemporary outlook), . . . [these considerations] entail not only that there isn't a God, but that the Divine Existence is either senseless or impossible." [47] And what is this "contemporary outlook" which makes the sentence 'There is a God' senseless? It is the position that "necessity in propositions merely reflects our use of words, the arbitrary conventions of our language".[48] In other words, since the sentence must be

[46]   *Ibid.*, p. 52.
[47]   *Ibid.*, p. 54. Brackets mine.
[48]   *Ibid.*, p. 54.

logically true and cannot be falsified by any contingent state-of-affairs, it asserts nothing whatsoever; it is senseless. This, you will remember, was Flew's criterion for meaningfulness: "If there is nothing which a putative assertion denies, then there is nothing which it asserts either: and so it is not really an assertion." [49]

It is quite crucial to see what Findlay and Flew are maintaining here. They are not erroneously arguing as Hume that no existential sentence can be necessary on the grounds that the negation of an existential sentence can never produce a contradiction. Nor are they, like Kant, limiting the category of existence and non-existence *ex cathedra* to possible objects given through the sensibility, among which they do not find God listed. Their argument rests solely on what Findlay has called "a contemporary outlook" and is taken to involve only the logical rules of language. It is the position that logically true sentences assert nothing but "merely reflect our use of words, the arbitrary conventions of our language". Once we have denied that the sentence 'There is a God' is a contingent sentence, then this is the dilemma which Findlay and a large portion of the analytic movement has presented to religious language: Either the concept of God is self-contradictory or it isn't. If it is self-contradictory, then the sentence 'There is a God' is logically false; and if the sentence, 'There is a God', is not false, then it is logically true and asserts nothing at all. Either God's existence is impossible or senseless.

I think we must agree with Findlay that the only being that could be considered an adequate object of the religious attitude of worship is the being treated in the argument from contingency and the ontological argument. Also, I think we must agree with Findlay that in both arguments the sentence 'There is a God' must be taken to be logically or necessarily true. For if the existence of God cannot be a contingent fact, then the sentence which asserts his existence cannot be a contingent sentence. We must, therefore, examine closely this "contemporary outlook", as Findlay calls it, which declares that a logically true sentence

[49]   *Ibid.*, p. 98.

is senseless and asserts nothing. This has brought us full circle back to the problem raised in connection with Braithwaite; that is, the need to re-examine the rules of descriptive discourse and the development of this so-called "contemporary outlook".

D. A PROPOSAL

It seems manifestly clear that a theory of religious language which takes at least some religious sentences as descriptive is to be preferred since some religious sentences used in the act of worship and in religious discourse concerning the act of worship are taken as descriptive by the users. In discussing the problem of a theory of religious discourse in connection with Braithwaite and Findlay, we suggested that any contemporary attempt to propose a descriptive theory must re-examine the rules of descriptive discourse and the so-called "contemporary outlook" as its first major problem. Chapter III will be primarily concerned with this problem. In connection with Braithwaite's non-descriptive theory we proposed as a major problem the need to examine religion and its language in order to determine the kinds of sentences that are taken as descriptive. This problem will be treated in Chapter IV along with Hick's problem of the kinds of truth conditions involved in religious statements. The other crucial problem suggested for a descriptive theory of religious discourse was the problem of characterizing a unique individual, or entity, named God. Chapters V, VI and VII will discuss the possibilities of characterizing an individual which can serve as an objective referent for religious discourse.

III

DESCRIPTIVE LANGUAGE, THE WORLD, AND NECESSITY

Toward the latter part of 1930, a new journal appeared on the philosophical scene. The introductory article was entitled: "The Turning Point in Philosophy". The turning point, according to the author, was to be the end of centuries of what he called "the fruitless conflict" of philosophic systems. He was quite optimistic: "We are already at the present", he wrote, "in possession of methods which make every such conflict in principle unnecessary".[1] What was to bring about this turning point? It was the realization that philosophy was not a system of cognitions, but "a system of acts". Philosophy was to be viewed as an activity, a method of logical analysis, through which the meaning of statements was revealed or determined. To quote the article: "By means of philosophy statements are explained, by means by science they are verified." Science "is concerned with the truth of statements"; philosophy "with what they actually mean".[2] The article closes with this prediction:

Certainly there will still be many a rear-guard action. Certainly many will for centuries continue to wander further along the traditional paths. Philosophical writers will long continue to discuss the old-pseudo-questions. But in the end they will no longer be listened to; they will come to resemble actors who continue to play for some time before noticing that the audience has slowly departed.[3]

The name of the new journal was *Erkenntnis*; the author of the article was Moritz Schlick; and this was the official introduction of logical positivism to the philosophic world.

[1] Moritz Schlick, "The Turning Point in Philosophy", *Logical Positivism*, edited by A. J. Ayer (Glencoe, Ill., Free Press, 1959), p. 54.
[2] *Ibid.*, p. 56.
[3] *Ibid.*, p. 59.

A. THE CONTRIBUTION OF LOGICAL POSITIVISM

The nucleus from which logical positivism, or logical empiricism, developed was the well-known Vienna Circle. This Circle evolved in 1923 out of a seminar led by Schlick at the University of Vienna. The most decisive period, according to Herbert Feigl,[4] one of the original members of the seminar, came in 1926 when Rudolph Carnap joined the faculty in Vienna and the Circle began a study of Ludwig Wittgenstein's *Tractatus Logico-Philosophicus*. The influence of these two men was formative. Under their influence the thinking of the group became crystallized, and by 1929 they were able to issue a joint manifesto entitled, "A Scientific World View: The Vienna Circle". Joergensen summarizes the basic aim, as set forth in the manifesto, in this way: "To further and propagate a scientific world view" by

... the use of the logical method of analysis, worked out by Peano, Frege, Whitehead and Russell, which serves to eliminate metaphysical problems and assertions as meaningless as well as to clarify the meanings of concepts and sentences of empirical science by showing their immediately observable content.[5]

This particular quote is significant for it gives, in a summary fashion, three of the tenets which are most commonly used to characterize logical positivism: a scientific world view through the unification of the empirical sciences, the elimination of traditional metaphysics, and a theory of meaning based on observation, or what has more commonly been formulated as the verifiability criterion of meaning. In fact, the general reading public is prone to identify logical positivism with the verifiability criterion of *Language, Truth and Logic*.[6] What has been even more unfortunate is the popular identification of the verifiability

---

[4] See H. Feigl, "Logical Empiricism", *Twentieth Century Philosophy*, edited by D. D. Runes (New York, Philosophical Library, 1943), pp. 406-8.
[5] J. Joergensen, "The Development of Logical Positivism", in *International Encyclopedia of Unified Science*, Vol. II, no. 9 (Chicago, University of Chicago Press, 1951), p. 4.
[6] A. J. Ayer, *Language, Truth and Logic*, p. 108.

criterion, and, consequently, logical positivism, with Ayer's emotive theory of ethical statements, the position that moral judgments are "pure expressions of feeling" and cannot be said to be either true or false.[7] As a result, logical positivism has often been condemned, like Socrates, as a corrupter of the morals of the youth.

The more scientifically minded, however, have naturally been attracted to logical positivism's attempt to unify the various empirical sciences into an overall scientific description of the world. Consequently, they have viewed logical positivism primarily as philosophy's long-over-due attempt to come of age and to develop a truly scientific philosophy. It is seen as the triumph of August Comte. On the other hand, those who see something in the scientific method which they would consider as alien to man's true nature tend to view such a scientific world view as demonic, as destructive of that which is truly human in man. The logical positivist, consequently, is characterized as a successor of Thomas Gradgrind in Dicken's *Hard Times*: "A man of facts and calculations. With a rule and a pair of scales, and the multiplication table always in his pocket, . . . ready to weigh and measure any parcel of human nature, and tell you exactly what it comes to."[8]

And then there have been those who, for one reason or another, have always been suspicious of the value of the traditional metaphysical speculations of philosophy. These, consequently, have been tempted to view logical positivism primarily as an attempt to eliminate metaphysics and to find in the movement a way to rid philosophy of this dreaded disease. On the other hand, those who feel at home in the speculations of traditional philosophy are most likely to characterize the movement as subversive and to view it as a traitor within the ranks of philosophy itself.

But whatever a person's reaction to these three tenets may be,

---

[7]   *Ibid.*, p. 108.
[8]   Charles Dickens, *Hard Times* (New York, The New American Library of World Literature, 1961), p. 12.

either pro or con, if he uses them to characterize logical positivism and evaluates the movement in terms of them, the score will not look good. For on all three accounts the movement could easily be judged as something of a failure. The attempt to formulate a criterion of meaning solely in terms of verifiability has been altered, revised, or outrightly rejected, by nearly every member of the Circle. Likewise, the original project for the unification of all the sciences now appears to have been a far too ambitious, if not impossible, task. For example, the *Journal of Unified Science* was discontinued shortly after it was begun, and the present *International Encyclopedia of Unified Science* seems to bear little resemblance to the original vision of the Vienna Circle. As for the elimination of metaphysics, by 1954 one of the original members of the group had published a book entitled, of all things, *The Metaphysics of Logical Positivism*,[9] in which he argued that logical positivism does not eliminate traditional metaphysics, rather it is a means of clarifying the disputes and aids in their solution. And when Carnap's article, "The Elimination of Metaphysics", originally published in 1932, was republished in 1957, he felt compelled to add the following footnote on his use of the term metaphysics in that article. He writes: "This term used in this paper ... includes systems like those of Fichte, Schelling, Hegel, Bergson, Heidegger. But it does not include endeavours toward a synthesis and generalization of the results of the various sciences." [10]

What then are we to say of logical positivism's contribution to philosophy? I do not think that the genius of logical positivism lies in these three tenets which are so commonly used to characterize the movement. Rather I think it is to be found in what Schlick referred to in his introductory article as the insight that philosophy was not a system of cognitions, but a system of acts and what the manifesto called the "logical method of analysis,

[9]   Gustav Bergmann, *The Metaphysics of Logical Positivism* (New York, Longmans, Green and Company, 1954).
[10]   Rudolf Carnap, "The Elimination of Metaphysics", *Logical Positivism*, edited by A. J. Ayer, p. 80.

worked out by Peano, Frege, Whitehead and Russell". The verifiability criterion of meaning, the idea of a scientific world view, and the distaste for metaphysics are all rooted in the old positivism of Comte and in traditional empiricism. But the genius of logical positivism was an attempt to wed these old ideas to a new conception of philosophy and a new method of logical analysis. This wedding is exemplified in the very names logical positivism and logical empiricism. But these new ideas have different roots. According to Schlick, "Leibniz saw their beginning, Bertrand Russell and Gottlob Frege opened up important stretches . . ., but Ludwig Wittgenstein in his *Tractatus* is the first to have pushed forward to the decisive turning point." [11]

In order to clarify this new conception of philosophy and its logical method of analysis, first, I want to examine Wittgenstein's *Tractatus* in order to determine the kind of analysis which he is doing. Secondly, I want to trace the development of some of these ideas in the work of Rudolph Carnap.

B.   WITTGENSTEIN AND THE *TRACTATUS*

It is generally agreed that the *Tractatus* is anything but easy to read. It is an unusual combination of logical precision and ineffable mysticism, of clear insight and inexcusable ambiguity. Here, however, we shall not be concerned with the details of the book, only with the main outline and the type of investigation which Wittgenstein is inaugurating. This, I think, is relatively clear. The work consists of seven cryptic aphorisms with a series of equally cryptic comments, all arranged and numbered in an elaborate system. The seven aphorisms are:

1.   The world is everything that is the case.
2.   What is the case, the fact, is the existence of atomic facts.
3.   The logical picture of the fact is the thought.

[11]   *Ibid.*, p. 54.

4. The thought is the significant proposition.
5. Propositions are truth-functions of elementary propositions.
6. The general form of truth-function is: (p, Z, N(Z)). This is the general form of proposition.
7. Whereof one cannot speak, thereof one must be silent.[12]

I want to raise the question: What is the problem with which Wittgenstein is concerned in these seven aphorisms? The order of the seven aphorisms gives the impression that he is beginning with the ontological question, What is there? But this is not the case; his starting point is not a directly intuited ontology, but a theory of meaning. As Russell puts it, he is attempting to answer the question, "What relation must one fact (such as a sentence) have to another to be capable of being a symbol for that other." [13] In other words, Wittgenstein is attempting to answer the question: What is the logical structure of descriptive language? Or, in more modern terms: What are the rules which govern the descriptive use of language? With all due respect to Wittgenstein's elaborately worked out order, the problem can, I think, be seen more clearly if we take the aphorisms in their reverse order.

Aphorism 7 is stated more fully in the "Preface": "Its whole meaning", he writes of the book, "can be summed up somewhat as follows: What can be said at all can be said clearly; and whereof one cannot speak, thereof he must be silent".[14] The other six aphorisms and their comments are designed to show what is involved in speaking clearly, that is, in making clear and precise true and false assertions about the world. Since it is by means of propositions, to use Wittgenstein's terminology, that we make true and false assertions, it is the structure of propositions and their relation to the world that Wittgenstein proposes

[12]   All quotes from the *Tractatus* are from the G. K. Ogden edition (London, Routledge and Kegan Paul, Ltd., 1955).
[13]   *Ibid.*, p. 8.
[14]   *Ibid.*, p. 27.

to analyze. And in order to understand what is involved in Wittgenstein's analysis, I think Schlick is quite right; we must go back to Leibniz to see "the beginning".

In the seventeenth century Leibniz conceived of a technique which he called the Combinatorial Art and which he hoped would reform all science. It consisted of a universal scientific language and a calculus of reasoning for the manipulation of the language. This conception of a universal language was based on the belief that all scientific predicates could be analyzed into a few primitive undefined predicates in terms of which all the other more complex conceptions of science could be defined. The calculus of reasoning, which was to be the structure of the language, consisted in the formulation of the rules of logic in a mathematical calculus. The purpose of this project was to provide a common language for all the sciences and to facilitate the process of logical deduction by substituting symbols for the words of ordinary language. It was, in fact, two centuries later that George Boole, an English mathematician, became the first to successfully reduce a part of logic to a complete and workable calculus. This work, along with the logical studies of Peirce and Schroeder, the axiomatic studies of arithmetic by Peano and the logical analyses of Frege, culminated in 1910-1913 in the publication by A. N. Whitehead and Bertrand Russell of the three volume classic in symbolic logic, *Principia Mathematica*.[15] Thus, a calculus of reasoning, which Leibniz had envisioned two hundred and fifty years earlier, became an accomplished fact. *Principia Mathematica* did not give Leibniz his primitive predicates in terms of which all the concepts of science could be defined, but it did give the logical structure of the propositions of any scientific theory plus the primitive concepts in terms of which virtually all the concepts of classical mathematics could be defined.

Although Wittgenstein rejected the development of mathematics in *Principia Mathematica,* it is the logical structure and

---

[15]   Bertrand Russell and A. N. Whitehead, *Principia Mathematica* (Cambridge, The University Press, 1910-1915).

the analysis of propositions developed there which lies behind Aphorisms 5 and 6 in the *Tractatus*. He took over from *Principia Mathematica* the division of propositions into atomic and molecular, and the thesis that molecular propositions are constructed from atomic propositions by the application of truth functional connectives. In 1913 H. M. Sheffer discovered that all the connectives could be defined in terms of only one connective, 'not both p and q' where 'p' and 'q' here stand for any propositions. It is this connective which Wittgenstein used to characterize what he calls the general truth function in Aphorism 6. All possible combinations of true and false propositions could be gotten by the successive application of this general truth function to atomic propositions, including, Wittgenstein maintained, universal and existential propositions. Thus, this general truth function is the general form of propositions, or the logical structure of propositions. And since the truth or falsity of all molecular propositions is determined by the truth or falsity of the atomic components, we have Aphorism 5: "The proposition is a truth function of elementary (or atomic) propositions."

Aphorisms 3 and 4 concern the relationship between propositions and what the propositions are about. The significant proposition, that is, the meaningful proposition is a thought, and a thought is a logical picture of a fact. But in order for the proposition to be a logical picture of a fact, it must have something in common with that fact. What the picture must have in common with that which it pictures is the logical form of representation. A photograph, for example, is a picture of a landscape because it has in common with the landscape a certain structure. A map is a picture of a particular area by virtue of having a structure in common with the area; it preserves, for example, the relationship between nations, mountains, rivers, seas, etc. Likewise, if we are to make true and false statements about the world, language must have in common with the world its logical structure; that is, the logical structure of propositions. To quote Wittgenstein: "To give the essence of propositions means to give the essence of all description, therefore the essence of the world" (5.4711).

Since a proposition pictures a fact, an elementary, or atomic proposition, pictures an atomic fact. And since all other propositions are but possible combinations of atomic facts, all possible facts are but combinations of atomic facts. Consequently, we have aphorisms 1 and 2. The world is everything that is the case, and what is the case is the existence of atomic facts. The world, then, is that which is pictured by all true atomic propositions.

In analyzing the structure of propositions, Wittgenstein found that a certain set of propositions will always be false regardless of the truth or falsity of the atomic propositions which compose it. For example, 'Socrates is mortal and it is not the case that Socrates is mortal', is false regardless of the atomic facts. These he called contradictions, and they picture no logically possible fact. Then there are those propositions which could be either true or false depending upon the truth or falsity of the components. These propositions are empirical propositions and picture logically possible facts and form the domain of the empirical sciences. It is the task of science, not philosophy, to determine their truth or falsity. But there is a third set of propositions: those propositions which are always true regardless of the truth or falsity of their atomic components. Take, for example, the proposition 'Socrates is mortal or it is not the case that Socrates is mortal'. This proposition is true independently of the atomic facts; it is logically true. Such propositions Wittgenstein labeled tautologies. Since they are true independently of the atomic facts, they assert nothing about the state of atomic facts, and, consequently, concludes Wittgenstein, they say nothing whatsoever about the world; that is, the world defined as atomic facts.

Although logically true propositions *say* nothing about the world, they do *show* something. They show the logical structure of the world. He writes: "The logical propositions describe the scaffolding of the world, or rather they present it" (6.124). But this logical structure itself cannot be talked about. "Propositions can represent the whole of reality, but they cannot represent what they must have in common with reality ... the logical form" (4.12). The reason for this is obvious. Propositions, as Wittgenstein has defined them, are things which are either true or false. A statement, however, which tells you about the structure of true and false propositions cannot be either true or false, for such statements would themselves presuppose that very structure. Consequently, we use the structure of propositions to assert things about the world, but we cannot assert anything about the structure itself. This structure, according to Wittgenstein, is "the inexpressible. This shows itself; it is the mystical" (6.522).

Such a position raises two obvious questions: First, if the task of philosophy is to analyze the structure of propositions and, yet, one cannot assert anything about the structure of propositions, where does that leave philosophy? "The object of philosophy", writes Wittgenstein, "is the logical clarification of thoughts. Philosophy is not a theory but an activity. ... The result of philosophy is not a number of 'philosophical propositions', but to make propositions clear" (4.112). The second obvious question which comes to mind is this: Is it not strange that Wittgenstein writes a book in which he certainly appears to talk about propositions and yet maintains that one cannot talk about propositions. Here again he has an answer. He simply says that his book is senseless. He concludes the *Tractatus* with this comment:

My propositions are elucidatory in this way: he who understands me finally recognizes them as senseless, when he has climbed out through them, on them, over them. [He must, so to speak, throw away the ladder, after he has climbed up on it.]
He must surmount these propositions; then he sees the world rightly (6.54).
Whereof one cannot speak, thereof one must be silent (7).

C. CARNAP AND THE *TRACTATUS*

Some members of the Vienna Circle, it appears, were not happy with Wittgenstein's resort to nonsense and his mystical turn at the end of the *Tractatus*. Carnap's development of Wittgenstein's conception of logical analysis can, I think, be viewed partially as an attempt to get around this problem. His first step was to take seriously a thesis advanced in the *Tractatus*, the thesis that all logically true propositions could be recognized by the form of the proposition alone. For example, Wittgenstein writes:

"It is the characteristic mark of logical propositions that one can perceive in the symbol alone that they are true; and this fact contains in itself the whole philosophy of logic" (6.113).

Thus, it seems that the rules of logic could be formulated without any reference whatsoever to what the symbols stand for. This, however, would mean that all the statements which refer to the relationship between statements and the world must be translated into rules which refer only to the symbols themselves. If this could be done, then the statements which Wittgenstein makes about this relationship could be eliminated, and with them a large part of the so-called "nonsense" of the *Tractatus*. This would mean that logic would be strictly formal, or as Alexander Maslow characterizes it: "Logic deals with rules and not with the reality to which the symbols may happen to refer." [16]

Carnap attempts to do this by translating statements in what he calls the material mode of speech – that is, statements which appear to talk about things – into statements in a formal mode which make no reference "either to the meaning of the symbols [for example, the words], or the sense of the expressions [for example, the sentence], but simply and solely to the kinds and orders of the symbols from which the expressions are constructed".[17] For example, one of Wittgenstein's comments in the *Tractatus* is: "The world is the totality of facts, not of things" (1.1). When this is translated into the formal mode by Carnap,

---

[16]   Alexander Maslow, *A Study in Wittgenstein's "Tractatus"* (Berkeley, University of California Press, 1961), p. 53.
[17]   Rudolf Carnap, *The Logical Syntax of Language*, translated by Amethe Smeaton (London, Routledge and Kegan Paul, Ltd., 1949), p. 1.

it becomes "Science is a system of sentences, not of names".[18] Thus, all reference to the world, facts or things is eliminated in the formal mode. Another sentence from the *Tractatus*, "If I know an object, then I also know all the possibilities of its occurrence in [atomic] facts" (2.0123), becomes when translated into the formal mode, "if the genus of a symbol is given then all the possibilities of its occurrence in sentences are also given".[19] Even such sentences as "The moon is a thing, five is not a thing, but a number" become when translated " 'Moon' is a thing-word; 'five' is not a thing-word, but a number-word." [20]

The second step toward an elimination of the so-called nonsense of the *Tractatus* was to demonstrate that all the formal rules which governed the symbols of a language could be stated in the language itself. This possibility would amount to a disproof of Wittgenstein's contention that the logical structure of a language could not be expressed in the language itself. Taking advantage of certain metamathematical studies of Hilbert and Goedel, Carnap was able to demonstrate this possibility in his *Logical Syntax of Language,* which he published in 1934. In this way the formal rules of a language become meaningful.

In this work Carnap also repudiated another, at least apparent, thesis of the *Tractatus*, the thesis that there is only one descriptive language. In the *Logical Syntax of Language* Carnap demonstrated that there are alternate sets of formal rules for descriptive language; consequently, which set one chooses becomes mere convention. There he proposes his "Principle of Tolerance": "Everyone is at liberty to build up his own logic, i.e., his own form of language, as he wishes. All that is required of him is that, if he wishes to discuss it, he must state his methods clearly, and give syntactical rules instead of philosophical arguments." [21]

Thus, in the *Logical Syntax of Language*, the senseless state-

---

[18] *Ibid.*, p. 303.
[19] *Ibid.*, p. 303.
[20] *Ibid.*, p. 297.
[21] *Ibid.*, p. 52.

ments and the mysticism of the *Tractatus* completely vanish. Philosophy is defined as the study of the formal properties of the languages of the empirical sciences. Logically true statements are true solely on the basis of the arbitrary, or conventional, rules which govern the kind and order of the symbols used in the statements made in the empirical sciences. This position could justifiably be called the classical position of logical positivism on logic and language. It is the work that lies behind, for example, much of Ayer's *Language, Truth and Logic*,[22] and the position which is frequently identified with logical positivism.

Only five years later, however, when Carnap published his *Foundations of Logic and Mathematics* (1939),[23] he had abandoned these three major theses. In all three cases he reverted to a position which is somewhat closer to the *Tractatus*. For he came to see that it was impossible to express all of what he took to be the logical properties of a language in strictly formal rules, ignoring the relationship between the symbols and what the symbols stand for. And largely under the influence of Tarski, Carnap in his later writings has developed a theory of logic which takes the semantic relationship, the relationship between the symbol and what the symbol stands for not only as necessary, but as basic. In his *Introduction to Semantics,* for example, he writes:

... the use of this method for the construction of a theory of truth by Tarski and its use in the present book for the construction of a theory of logical deduction and a theory of interpretation of formal systems seems to justify the expectation that semantics will not only be of accidental help to pure logic but will supply the basis for it.[24]

This apparent reversal by Carnap is significant and the reasons for it are very important. He repudiated the thesis that the logical

[22]   In the "Preface", for example, Ayer in stating his indebtedness to the Vienne Circle writes: "I owe most to Rudolf Carnap" (p. 32).
[23]   Rudolf Carnap, *Foundations of Logic and Mathematics* in *International Encyclopedia of Unified Science*, Vol. 1, no. 3 (Chicago, University of Chicago Press, 1939).
[24]   Rudolf Carnap, *Introduction to Semantics* (Cambridge, Harvard University Press, 1942), p. viii.

properties of a language could be fully expressed in formal, or purely syntactical, rules for several reasons. For one thing, Carnap recognized that semantical rules were, in fact, implicit in the logical analysis which he and his contemporaries were doing. "Some essential features", he writes, "in the contemporary work of logicians are guided by instinct and common sense, although they could be guided by explicit rules. These rules, however, would be not syntactical but semantical." [25] When one reads, for example, the attempt in *The Logical Syntax of Language* to construct a purely syntactical set of rules, he cannot help but feel that it is a *tour de force*. To translate, for example, a statement such as 'The moon is a thing; five is not a thing, but a number' into the statement " 'Moon' is a thing-word; 'five' is not a thing-word, but a number-word", is not to eliminate semantics, it is merely to disguise the relation between the symbol and what it stands for.

Another reason for the rejection of the purely formalistic programs proposed in *The Logical Syntax of Language* is the fact that certain logical problems cannot be treated in a purely syntactical system. In the *Formalization of Logic*, Carnap points to the fact that the question as to whether or not a proposed calculus formalizes a given theory adequately and completely cannot be treated in pure syntax; "it is a matter of the relations between a calculus and an interpreted system, and hence requires semantics in addition to syntax." [26] But an even more important problem, perhaps, is the problem of the distinction between logically true statements, which are dependent solely upon the semantical rules for the determination of their truth value, and factually true statements, which, in addition, are dependent upon the contingent facts for the determination of their truth value. The distinction here is a distinction which, Carnap writes, "is indispensable for the logical analysis of science".[27]

[25] *Ibid.*, p. xi.
[26] Rudolf Carnap, *Formalization of Logic* (Cambridge, Harvard University Press, 1943), p. vii.
[27] Carnap, *Introduction to Semantics*, p. viii.

This rejection of the formalistic thesis forced Carnap to abandon his other two theses. All the rules which Carnap now considered as logical rules could no longer be formulated in the language itself. But this was unimportant since rules are not taken as asserting true and false statements. Likewise he was forced to abandon his thesis that the logical rules of a language were merely arbitrary, or conventional. For when one considers the subject matter of a language, he finds that the logical rules which govern the language can no longer be strictly arbitrary. The subject matter imposes certain restrictions.[28] These developments have subsequently led Carnap to divide the logical analysis of the rules of descriptive language into three different sets: the rules of syntax, the rules of semantics, and the rules of pragmatics. The most obvious thing about a descriptive language is that it is a group of symbols which stand *for* something *for* somebody. Thus, one may study a language purely from the perspective of the rules which govern the relationship between the symbols themselves without any reference to what they stand for or the user of the symbols. These rules are the syntactical rules and they govern the proper formation of sentences and the logical rules of inference. On the other hand, one might study a language from the perspective of the rules which govern the relationships between the symbols and what they stand for. These are the semantical rules, and they include rules for the interpretation of the symbols and rules for the determination of the truth or falsity of the sentences, including both logical and factual sentences. Thirdly, one can study a language from the perspective of the rules which govern and express the relationships between the symbols and the users of the symbols. These rules are called pragmatic rules and they govern such relationships as 'believes', 'accepts', 'verifies', or 'knows'. For example, 'I believe the statement, "Socrates is mortal", to be true' expresses a relationship between me and the statement 'Socrates is mortal'.

[28]   See Carnap, *Foundations of Logic and Mathematics*, pp. 26ff.

D. THE "CONTEMPORARY OUTLOOK"

In his introductory remarks to "Theology and Falsification", Antony Flew proposes the following criterion for distinguishing assertive statements: "If there is nothing which a putative assertion denies then there is nothing which it asserts either: and so it is not really an assertion." [29] In support of his criterion, Flew calls our attention to the well-known logical principle that a statement is logically equivalent to the denial of its negation; that is, p is logically equivalent to ∼p. Flew, however, seems to mean more by his criterion for assertive statements than this simple logical principle. For in his application of the criterion to theological statements, he poses for the theologian the following question: "What would have to occur or to have occurred to constitute for you disproof of the love of, or of the existence of, God?" [30] In raising this question, Flew is certainly going far beyond the simple logical rule that a statement is logically equivalent to the denial of its negation; there is implicit in this question an additional condition for assertive statements beyond this simple logical principle. The further implicit condition in Flew's question is that the negation of an assertion must be a contingent statement, for he is, in fact, asking for a possible occurrence, or a possible contingent state of affairs, as a condition for the falsification of an assertive statement. In other words, in the actual application of his criterion for assertive statements, Flew is in fact saying, "If there is no contingent fact which a putative assertion denies then there is nothing which it asserts either: and so it is not really an assertion." It is easy now to see the consequences of Flew's criterion; necessary statements assert nothing. Since no contingent fact can falsify a necessary statement, then it follows, according to Flew's criterion, that necessary statements assert nothing.

J. N. Findlay, in the discussion, "Can God's Existence be

---

[29] Flew and MacIntyre, *New Essays in Philosophical Theology*, p. 98.
[30] *Ibid.*, p. 99.

Disproved?", is far more explicit on the non-assertive character of necessary statements; he writes: "necessity in propositions merely reflects our use of words, the arbitrary conventions of our language." [31] Necessary statements, according to him, are "senseless"; [32] and by calling them "senseless" he seems to mean the same thing as Flew does when he tells us that they assert nothing. This position that necessary statements "assert nothing" and merely reflect "our use of words, the arbitrary conventions of our language" is so prevalent in contemporary philosophy that it has been christened by Findlay as "the contemporary outlook".

This position, or outlook, may be shared by many contemporary philosophers, but it is far from new. One of the clearest expressions of it is found in Hobbes' Fourth Objection to Descartes' *Meditations*. In his fourth objection, Hobbes makes this proposal to Descartes:

> ... what shall we say, if reasoning chance to be nothing more than the uniting and stringing together of names or designations by the word is? It will be a consequence of this that reason gives us no conclusions about the nature of things, but only about the terms that designate them, whether, indeed, or not there is a convention (arbitrarily made about these meanings) according to which we join these names together.[33]

When Hobbes proposes that "reason gives us no conclusions about the nature of things", he seems to be suggesting, as Flew, that necessary statements assert nothing; and when he proposes that reason gives us conclusions "only about the terms that designate them, whether ... or not there is a convention" he seems to be suggesting, with Findlay, that necessary statements merely reflect "our use of words, the arbitrary conventions of our language".

---

[31]   *Ibid.*, p. 54.
[32]   *Ibid.*, p. 54.
[33]   *The Complete Works of Descartes*, translated by Elizabeth S. Holdane and G. R. T. Ross (Cambridge, Cambridge University Press, 1958) and reprinted in Walter Kaufman, *Philosophic Classics* (Englewoood Cliffs, Prentice-Hall, Inc., 1961), I, p. 80.

It is not the purpose of this discussion either to refute the view that necessary statements are non-assertive or to defend their assertive character. In fact, I do not think that it is quite clear exactly what either a refutation or a defense would be. I do think, however, a strong case can be made that this so-called "contemporary outlook", at least as expressed by Flew, Findlay and Hobbes, is quite ambiguous, if not confused and misleading.

In order to limit our discussion, let me specify a set of statements which most would classify as necessary statements. Let us take those statements whose truth or falsity can be determined solely on the basis of the rules of the classical first order predicate logic and a relevant set of definitions as our set of necessary statements. I do not intend to suggest that I would limit necessary statements to this group, but this minimum set is sufficient for our purposes. The statement, 'Socrates is mortal or it is not the case that Socrates is mortal', and the statement, 'Nothing is both red and not red', would both be necessary statements, since we can determine them to be true solely on the basis of the rules of the first order predicate logic. Likewise, the statement, 'All bachelors are unmarried', is a necessary statement since we can determine its truth value solely on the basis of the rules of the first order predicate logic and the customary definition of 'bachelor'.

In the light of this particular group of statements, what could one mean by the phrases, 'asserts nothing', 'merely reflects our use of words', 'the arbitrary conventions of our language?' First, consider the phrase, 'asserts nothing'. It seems that one could mean one of two things by it: He might, for example, mean that the symbols in the statement are uninterpreted. This seems to be the way in which Descartes interpreted Hobbes' fourth objection, for he asks, ". . . if he admits that words signify anything, why will he not allow our reasonings to refer to this something that is signified, rather than to words alone?" [34] One can seriously question, on the grounds of the customary usage of the word,

---

[34] *Ibid.*, p. 81.

'statement', the propriety of calling an uninterpreted string of symbols a statement. Be that as it may; it is quite clear that if one has semantical rules governing the interpretation of the symbols appearing in a necessary statement, then that statement has an interpretation. Here the implications of Descartes' question are sound: If one gives an interpretation to the predicate 'red' and the ordinary interpretation to the quantifiers and connectives in first order predicate calculus, then the necessary statement, 'Nothing is both red and not red', is certainly an interpreted statement. Thus, if the proponents of the contemporary view, when they maintain that necessary statements assert nothing, mean that necessary statements are uninterpreted, then they are quite wrong.

An alternative way of interpreting the phrase, 'asserts nothing', would be to interpret it as meaning 'asserts no contingent fact'. Under this rendering, however, the proponents of the contemporary outlook would merely be maintaining that a necessary statement does not assert a contingent state-of-affairs. But this would be trivial, in the sense that no one would question it. It is obvious that Flew, Findlay and Hobbes want to say more than this. It is to give expression to this "more" that Findlay proposes that "necessity in propositions merely reflects our use of words, the arbitrary conventions of our language"; and Hobbes proposes that reason gives us conclusions "only about terms . . . whether . . . or not there is a convention . . . according to which we join these names together". Here again, however, we are faced with ambiguity. What could one mean when he tells us that a necessary statement "merely reflects our use of words" or "gives us conclusions only about words". One might mean that the statement asserts something about words or terms rather than about extra-linguistic entities. Again, this seems to be the way in which Descartes interpreted Hobbes; for example, he answers: ". . . in reasoning we unite not names but the things signified by names; and I marvel that the opposite can occur to anyone." [35]

---

[35]   *Ibid.*, p. 81.

If modern studies in language systems have taught us anything, they have taught us to distinguish clearly when we are talking about linguistic entities and when we are talking about non-linguistic entities. Take, for example, the assertion that the statement, 'Socrates is mortal', is either true or false. Such an assertion is clearly about a linguistic entity, namely, a statement, and such an assertion would be in our meta-language. On the other hand, the assertion, 'Socrates is mortal or it is not the case that Socrates is mortal', is clearly a statement about a non-linguistic entity, namely, Socrates. Now if our proponents of the contemporary view are maintaining that necessary statements are solely about linguistic entities, then they are quite wrong.

If our proponents, however, are not confusing meta-language and object language statements, what do they mean by "merely reflects our use of words?" What seems to lie behind this phrase is the fact that the truth values of necessary statements seem to be dependent on our logical rules and definitions, whereas the truth values of contingent statements seem to be dependent upon contingent facts. This is the fact which seems to lie behind the use of such words as 'arbitrary' and 'conventional' when used in reference to necessary statements. Now in a sense, this is, of course, true; but the sense in which it is true needs to be made quite clear. It is quite true that if one defined the word 'bachelor' quite differently from its customary definition, which is certainly a convention and, in this sense, arbitrary, then the string of symbols, 'All bachelors are unmarried', may not then even be true but it would also be an entirely different statement. It needs to be pointed out, however, that our contingent statements are likewise dependent upon our logical rules and definitions. For it is also the case that the string of symbols 'Fifty per cent of our contemporary bachelors are blackheaded', might change its truth value, if our customary definition of bachelor were changed, but it, too, would be an entirely different statement. It is not the case that necessary statements are dependent upon conventional rules and definitions whereas contingent statements are not. Contingent

statements are dependent upon the very same rules and definitions. Consequently, necessary statements are no more arbitrary
and conventional, in this sense, than are contingent statements.

What is the sense in which necessary statements are dependent
upon our logical rules and definitions and the sense in which
contingent statements are dependent upon contingent facts? Merely
this: the logical rules and definitions are sufficient for determining
the truth values of necessary statements, whereas one must take
into account additional extra-logical considerations, namely, contingent facts, in order to determine the truth value of contingent
statements. But this is merely to say that contingent facts are
irrelevant to the truth value of necessary statements or that necessary statements are not contingent statements.

Thus, it seems that when someone like Findlay maintains that
a necessary statement "merely reflects our use of words, the
arbitrary conventions of our language", he seems to be saying
either that the truth value of a necessary statement is dependent
upon arbitrary rules and definitions, whereas the truth value of
a contingent statement is solely dependent upon extra-logical
facts; or that a contingent statement needs additional non-logical
facts in order to determine its truth value, whereas a necessary
statement does not. If he is maintaining the first, then he is quite
wrong; if he is maintaining the second, then he is only maintaining
the obvious and no one would argue with him.

I do not think, however, that a proponent of the view that
necessary statements "assert nothing" would be satisfied with
this analysis, for he would like to say that there is still a sense
in which necessary statements assert nothing; they are trivial in
a way in which contingent statements are not. Necessary statements seem to add nothing to our contingent knowledge of the
world; contingent statements do. To assert the statement, 'Socrates is mortal or it is not the case that Socrates is mortal',
seems to add nothing to one's knowledge about Socrates. To
assert the statement, 'Nothing is both red and not red', seems to
tell me nothing new about the universe. And certainly the state-

ment, 'All bachelors are unmarried', tells us nothing new about bachelors. There are two problems which must be considered here: 1) If necessary statements are assertive, what do they assert? and 2) If necessary statements are assertive, in what way are they trivial?

If one maintains, as I think most would, that a logically in-determinate statement asserts a contingent state-of-affairs – one which may or may not be the case, depending upon the actual state of the world – then it would certainly seem intelligible to say that a logically false statement asserts an impossible state-of-affairs – one that could not possibly be the case, no matter what the actual state of the world is – and that a logically true state-ment asserts a necessary state-of-affairs – one that could not be otherwise, no matter what the actual state of the world is. As for the second question, the question of the triviality of necessary statements, this is, I think, not basically a logical problem but a problem of value judgments. And when one tells us that necessary statements are trivial, is he not merely telling us that they are unimportant? And if one is primarily interested in adding infor-mation concerning contingent facts to his accumulation of knowl-edge, then certainly necessary statements can be judged as trivial and unimportant. But, as Charles Hartshorne has suggested,[36] there may be some factually empty but important truths in rela-tion to some other purpose. Whether this is the case or not, the decision as to their triviality or non-triviality is a decision about their value, not one as to whether or not they assert anything.

E.   THE A PRIORI-SYNTHETIC REFORMULATED

Perhaps the problem of the distinction between necessary and contingent statements will become clearer if we return to the task of philosophy as formulated by the Vienna Circle. We suggested

---

[36]   See Charles Hartshorne, *The Logic of Perfection* (LaSalle, Open Court Publishing Company, 1962), pp. 280-297.

that this task, as presented in the *Tractatus,* was the task of investigating the rules of descriptive discourse – that is, the language we use in describing the common world disclosed to us in experience. We concluded this discussion with Carnap's distinction between syntactical, semantical and pragmatical rules. Such a set of rules will be referred to as a linguistic framework. In the light of this task and these rules, let us look at the problem of necessary and contingent statements.

In the *Critique of Pure Reason*, Kant speaks of an a priori judgment in this way: "If . . . a judgment is thought with strict universality, that is, in such a manner that no exception is allowed as possible, it is not derived from experience, but is valid *a priori*." [37] I quote this not to seek the support of Kant, nor to get involved in his epistemology, but to suggest a parallel here between the phrase, "no exception is allowed as possible", and Flew's question, "What would have to occur or to have occurred to constitute for you a disproof . . .?" In both cases the key to the necessity of a judgment or statement lies in the irrelevancy of particular events or occurrences to the determination of its truth or falsity. Let us say, then, that a statement is taken as a priori, or necessary, if there are no particular occurrences or events which would be considered as relevant to the determination of its truth or falsity; whereas, a statement is taken as a posteriori, or contingent, if there are events or occurrences which would be considered as relevant to the determination of its truth or falsity. What is important here is that this distinction is made in terms of what will be allowed in the determination of the truth or falsity; that is, in terms of what we would allow to count in the justification for accepting or holding the statement as true or false. As such this distinction between necessity and contingency is a distinction made at the level of pragmatics, not at the level of semantics.

In relation to this distinction, let us consider another traditional distinction made famous by Kant, the distinction between analytic

[37] Immanuel Kant, *Critique of Pure Reason*, translated by Norman K. Smith (London, Macmillan and Company, Ltd., 1963), p. 44.

and synthetic statements. Although Kant's manner of distinguishing between analytic and synthetic judgments is of little use in
contemporary logic, I think it could justifiably be claimed that it
is an attempt to make, in contemporary terminology, a distinction
at the level of semantics, for his distinction has to do with meaning in the sense of the interpretation of the symbols. More recent
attempts to give a more precise distinction in terms of contemporary logic do make this distinction a semantic one.[38] Although
one needs a particular linguistic framework or semantic theory
in order to give a precise distinction, we can say that most definitions of analyticity are formulated so that the class of analytic
statements includes those statements and only those statements
which are true in virtue of the semantical interpretation of the
logical connectives, the quantifiers and identity. All other statements are taken as synthetic.

With these distinctions in mind, let us for the moment suppress
Kant's question, How are synthetic propositions a priori possible,
and ask: What kinds of statements appear as candidates for this
class of a priori-synthetic statements? If a linguistic framework
includes a set of axioms for mathematics, such as set theory or
class theory, then we would have a set of true statements which
would fall into this class. These statements would be a priori,
for we allow no events or occurrences to count either for or
against their truth, and, at the same time, they would fail to
qualify as analytic. But the major task of the metaphysician has
been to concern himself with the question as to whether or not
there are other a priori-synthetic statements. In other words, are
there statements, other than those of mathematics, which are
taken as true of any and every event? If so, it would seem that
they would be those statements which express the defining characteristics of an event or occurrence – in effect, they would be

[38]   See A. Tarski, *Logic, Semantics, Metamathematics* (Oxford, Clarendon
Press, 1956), pp. 409-20; R. Carnap, *Introduction to Semantics, passim*;
R. Martin, *The Notion of Analytic Truth* (Philadelphia, University of
Pennsylvania Press, 1959).

those statements which give expression to what we mean by the phrase, "the common world disclosed to us in experience". In a linguistic framework, such as we have suggested, these statements, along with the analytic statements and the mathematical statements, would constitute the necessary statements – those statements which would, as Leibniz suggests, be true of any possible world.

In effect this is the conception of a descriptive framework taken in the *Tractatus*. For example, Aphorism 1 tells us what Wittgenstein takes to be the actual world; namely, everything that is the case. Aphorism 2 tells us that what is the case, the world, is atomic facts. Since atomic facts are pictured in atomic statements and all statements are truth functions of atomic statements, it follows that what would be true of all possible worlds is shown in the structure of the truth functional logic. Tautologies become precisely those statements which would be true of all possible worlds and consequently tell us nothing in particular about this actual world, the atomic facts. Thus, Stuart Hampshire can justifiably call the *Tractatus* an "attempt at a metaphysical system" [39] and place it in the "tradition of philosophical writings which effectively begins with Aristotle and passes through Aquinas and others in the Middle Ages, comes to life again in Descartes, Spinoza and Leibniz, suffers an enormous change in Kant, and continues in this century in the early work of Russell".[40]

The inadequacy, however, of Wittgenstein's development of quantification theory and mathematics is well known and indicates that we must go beyond the axioms of propositional logic and include the axioms of quantification theory and some form of set theory or class theory in order to have an adequate linguistic framework for describing the common world. The crucial metaphysical question then becomes, how adequate is such an

---

[39]   Stuart Hampshire, "Metaphysical Systems", *The Nature of Metaphysics*, edited by D. F. Pears (London, Macmillan and Company, Ltd., 1957), p. 26.
[40]   *Ibid.*, p. 29.

amended framework? Must we not have additional extra-logical and extra-mathematical axioms in order to adequately characterize what we mean by the common world disclosed to us in experience? The development of this kind of task was undertaken by Carnap in *Der Logische Aufbau der Welt* [41] and by Nelson Goodman in *The Structure of Appearance*.[42] But two serious questions remain: How can one attempt be judged more adequate than another? How does one answer Kant's question: How are synthetic propositions a priori possible? These questions will be discussed in Chapter VI.

After thirty years, when one looks back at the optimism in Schlick's introductory article, "The Turning Point in Philosophy", his optimism certainly appears excessive. Philosophic conflict has not vanished. Nevertheless, it has been the contribution of logical positivism and the development of its insight to recall philosophy to one of its major tasks and to give philosophy some effective tools for attempting this task in the twentieth century. The aim and the method of logical analysis which was suggested in the *Tractatus* and which formed the inspiration for the Vienna Circle leads one to raise once again the question of those necessarily true statements which would form the necessary framework for a language adequate for describing the common world disclosed to us in experience. It may be the irony of philosophy in the twentieth century that the movement which began as an attempt to eliminate metaphysics has perhaps succeeded in recalling philosophy to this traditional task and suggested tools with which to work more effectively.

[41]   Rudolf Carnap, *Der Logische Aufbau der Welt* (Leipzig, F. Meiner, 1928).
[42]   Nelson Goodman, *The Structure of Appearance* (Cambridge, Harvard University Press, 1951).

IV

REVELATION, NATURAL THEOLOGY, AND LANGUAGE

In his essay entitled, "A Starting-Point for the Philosophical Examination of Theological Belief", Austin Farrer states the impact of modern linguistic philosophy upon theology in this way:

The old method of philosophizing about theology was the endeavor to prove. This meant to prove theological conclusions from non-theological premises. . . . Such a method of proceeding is now out of fashion.[1]

In the essay he goes on to express a position which might be called "linguistic pluralism"; that is, the position that "every science, art, or manner of speaking is now supposed to find its own justification in its own use".[2] This theory of linguistic pluralism leads Farrer to conclude that "in such a philosophical climate the difference of status . . . between the demonstrable and the indemonstrable parts of theology, between 'rational' and 'revealed' doctrines largely disappears".[3]

Farrer's position here may be summarized in two main points: First, modern developments in logic and methodology have necessitated a plurality of language systems; for example, a language of science, a language of morals, a language of art, a language of religion, with each language obeying different logical rules and finding its own justification in its own use. Secondly, these developments necessitate a radical distinction between religious language with its own system of symbols and their use and any other language, such as the language of science. As a result, the distinction between revealed and rational theology disappears

---

[1] Mitchell, *Faith and Logic*, p. 9.
[2] *Ibid.*, p. 9.
[3] *Ibid.*, p. 10.

and with it the hope of justifying any theological doctrines on non-theological grounds.

In the earlier chapters I have argued that modern attempts to treat the language of religious doctrine as something other than descriptive discourse, whether it be emotive language, moral discourse, or even something entirely unique, have failed. For it seems to me quite clear that, at least in the Christian tradition, doctrinal expressions have generally been taken as describing states-of-affairs and not as expressing emotions, or as disguised moral statements, or as merely stating an intention to lead a particular way of life. To propose such a theory is simply to say that people have been using language in a way in which they themselves would deny. In this chapter we shall examine first the nature of revelation and the traditional role of natural theology; then we shall raise the question of the possibility of the descriptive character of the doctrines of revelation and natural theology. I must, however, emphasize that I am limiting myself to a treatment of the Christian tradition only and limiting myself solely to the methodological problem. In other words, I shall not be concerned with the truth or falsity of any theological doctrine. This is the theologian's concern; the logician's concern is solely with methodology, the conditions under which theological doctrines may be taken as descriptive statements.

A. THE NATURE OF REVELATION

The conception of revelation, in some form or other, is as old and widespread as the idea of God or religion itself, and it is universally accepted as the fundamental basis of religion and religious truth. As Dawson points out, "This holds good for all the historic religions: everywhere revelation is regarded as the primary source of religious truth, and intuition and reason are secondary."[4] Yet when one examines historical Christianity, he

---

[4] Christopher Dawson, *Religion and Culture* (New York, Meridian Books, 1958), p. 43.

can find no standard or authoritative definition of the word revelation. In fact, neither in the Old Testament nor the New Testament do we find a word which corresponds to the theological conception of revelation. There is only a record of what might be called revelatory events; God acts or speaks and there is a seeing and a hearing. The Bible, as Brunner tells us, always "points beyond itself to an event to which it bears witness".[5] In a sense, the same thing might be said for Christian doctrine. Tillich is quite true to the history of the formation of Christian doctrine when he writes: "There are no revealed doctrines, but there are revelatory events and situations which can be described in doctrinal terms."[6] Thus, in order to determine the nature of Christian revelation, one must examine the nature of the revelatory events which form part of its tradition.

As the term revelation, 'removing the veil', would indicate, in a revelatory event something is disclosed to somebody; and that which is disclosed is taken to be God in some particular manifestation or relation. As Tillich defines it, a revelatory event "is an event which points to the mystery of being, expressing its relation to us in a definite way".[7] It necessarily involves its particular reception and particular mode of reception by a particular person or persons. When taken in abstraction from its reception – that is, as it might appear to any, and yet, no particular observer – the event, whatever else it might be, ceases to be a revelatory event. Thus, Tillich is justified in saying: "The Christ is not the Christ without the church, and the church is not the church without the Christ."[8]

This insistence upon the particularity and concreteness of revelatory events naturally points to the uniqueness of the events. God is not manifested in the general aspect of the event, that is,

[5] Emil Brunner, *Revelation and Reason*, translated by Olive Wyon (Philadelphia, The Westminster Press, 1956), p. 12.
[6] Paul Tillich, *Systematic Theology* (Chicago, University of Chicago, 1951), I, 125.
[7] *Ibid.*, I, p. 117.
[8] *Ibid.*, I, p. 137.

that which an event might have in common with other events, but precisely in that which distinguishes it from all other events – its uniqueness and novelty. It is for this reason that revelatory events have the quality of mystery and the unexpected, and revelation has the character of being given. As Brunner points out, "the truths which the intellect can perceive are in principle always at our disposal", but revelation, which concerns "the unique . . . that which can never be repeated", comes as "a gift, a 'disclosure', which we could not have expected".[9]

This particular and concrete nature of revelatory events may be seen in another dimension. Despite the fact that they always involve the receiver and emphasize the unique, they never occur in isolation, but always in a particular society, in a particular epoch, and conditioned by particular antecedents. As Reinhold Niebuhr writes: "The revelation of God to man is always a twofold one, a personal-individual revelation and a revelation in the context of social-historical experience."[10] There is always that communal background of commitments, values, and memories of past revelatory events. This is true even of the mystic's experience. Perhaps here the conscious relation to the community is at a minimum, but it is nonetheless there in the background with its particular traditions and memories. It is this contrast between the uniqueness of the revelatory event and its context of traditions and memories which gives the revelatory events the dramatic structure which H. R. Niebuhr has characterized in this way: "how our present grows out of our past and into our future."[11] And it is this contrast between the novel and the traditional which, at least in part, gives the Bible its dramatic structure of judgment and redemption; its prophet and its priest.

Since revelatory events never occur in isolation but within a

---

[9]   Brunner, pp. 29-30.
[10]   Reinhold Niebuhr, *Nature and Destiny of Man* (London, Hishet and Company, 1944), I, p. 127.
[11]   H. R. Niebuhr, *The Meaning of Revelation* (New York, Macmillan and Co., 1941), p. 128.

dramatic structure, they cannot be judged in isolation but as parts of one organic and dramatic whole. This standard of organic and dramatic unity becomes the standard whereby events are judged both as to their validity and relative importance. In this sense Tillich is right; the validity of a revelatory event "is not dependent on criteria which are not themselves revelatory".[12] And for this reason Brunner, when writing of the revelatory events of the Bible, says:

It is true, of course, that not all the ways in which events and ideas are presented in the Bible, to which "revealed" significance is ascribed, are of the same organic importance within the whole; but they are all related to the whole; none is without significance for the understanding of the whole.[13]

These revelatory events, which when taken as a whole form an organic and dramatic unity, can be termed 'the revelation'.

Revelatory events are not taken to be mere passive disclosures; they are efficacious and have a significance beyond themselves. "In the history of religion", writes Tillich, "revelatory events always have been described as shaking, transforming, demanding, significant in some ultimate way." [14] Of course, the ultimate significance or intended efficacy of the Christian revelation is the salvation of man. Its purpose is not to add anything to our knowledge of the general nature of the universe, but to do something, to transform, to create. In the words of Brunner, "it does not make me 'educated'; it does not enlarge my 'sphere', but it transforms *me myself*; it changes the one who receives it".[15]

The efficacy of these revelatory events is extended beyond the memories of those who receive them by language. Thus as H. R. Niebuhr points out,

The preaching of the early Christian Church ... was primarily a simple recital of the great events connected with the historical appear-

[12]   Tillich, I, p. 131.
[13]   Brunner, p. 22.
[14]   Tillich, I, p. 110.
[15]   Brunner, p. 27.

ance of Jesus Christ and a confession of what had happened to the community of his disciples. Whatever the Church meant to say, whatever was revealed or manifested to it could be indicated only in connection with an historical person and events in the life of his community.[16]

These events were recorded in order that their efficacy might be extended beyond the memories of those that received them into the life of a continuing historical community. But the language used was adapted to the purpose of both recording and extending their efficacy. What was pointed to, or indicated, was the uniqueness felt in these particular events; there was no attempt to describe them as they might appear to just any observer. There is no use of general terms, pointing to what this event has in common with other events of the same type. The symbols employed are used to evoke concrete images which have what Whitehead calls, "the implicit suggestion of the concrete unity of experience".[17] The language of abstract description is inadequate to express their uniquenes and the inexhaustible richness of their concreteness. Nor is their purpose to describe; it is to continue the efficacy of the revelatory events beyond their immediate efficacy. Consequently, the words employed and the images evoked are those which have been emotionally charged through their continued use within the religious life of the community. In this way, the hearer, as Wright suggests, "listens to the recital and by means of historical memory and identification he participates, so to speak, in the original events".[18] In so far as the language of revelation is concerned, Ramsey is right when he writes that its "characteristic point is to evoke a distinctly personal situation".[19]

Since the symbols used in the language of the record of revelation evoke concrete images and the events pointed to form an

[16]   H. R. Niebuhr, p. 43.
[17]   A. N. Whitehead, *Essays in Science and Philosophy* (New York, Macmillan and Co., 1926), p. 112.
[18]   G. E. Wright, *God Who Acts* (London, S.C.M. Press, 1952), p. 28.
[19]   Ramsey, *Religious Language*, pp. 38-39.

organic and dramatic unity, the structure, as well as the symbols, of the language is poetic and dramatic. For this reason, H. R. Niebuhr tells us that to think in the language of revelation is "to think with poets rather than with scientists".[20] This is not to say revelation is poetry. Such an identification would be misleading unless the meaning of 'poetry' were qualified. It is only to say that the structure of the language of revelation is the structure of *mythos* rather than *logos*. And because of this structure, the sentences composing the record of revelation cannot be isolated and verified, any more than a sentence can be isolated from a drama and verified.

B.   THE ROLE OF NATURAL THEOLOGY

In contrast to this concrete and particular aspect of religion, what can be said for that aspect which has generally been called natural theology and which deals with general ideas and connects religion with the rational generality of philosophy? If revelation, as outlined, deals with particular relations or manifestations of God disclosed in the uniqueness of certain revelatory events, involving both a particular reception and a particular communal context, there will be that aspect which can be said to deal with God as related to, or manifested in, any and every event without reference to any particular individual or community. This is the area of natural theology. This does not mean, of course, that natural theology can exist without some particular community. It is always developed within a particular community and influenced by that community, but it can be formulated and judged without reference to the particular revelatory events of any particular community.

There is also a difference of purpose in these two aspects of religion. Whereas the purpose of revelation is to make God efficacious within the lives of particular men and particular com-

[20]   H. R. Niebuhr, p. 71.

munities, the purpose of natural theology is to connect religion through its general ideas to philosophy, particularly to that area of philosophy which deals with the most general categories of existence – metaphysics. As Maritain writes, "all metaphysical knowledge, including the knowledge of God, is knowledge in terms of being in general".[21] Thus, since natural theology concerns God's relation to events in general, it overlaps metaphysics and forms a part of its subject matter.

It is through these general ideas and their inclusion within a metaphysics that religion can find its connection with the rest of the intellectual life of the community. Even Zuurdeeg, who considers metaphysics to be "a misuse of language" and a "confusion of its functions',[22] seeks this connection. He tells us that the indicative language of science, for example, is "based upon a set of presuppositions and assumptions which are convictional in nature"[23] and that our convictional languages, among which is theological language, "form more or less a coherent whole".[24] If there is any other way in which such a schema can be worked out except by a metaphysics, it has yet to be found. Although one may not agree with Dawson that "the breach of communion between the spiritual and the rational order is the most formidable problem that confronts the modern world", one must agree that if it is a problem, "the recognition of the function of Natural Theology is one of the necessary conditions for its solution".[25]

C. PHILOSOPHICAL PROOFS FOR GOD

Whether one agrees that the God of Abraham, Isaac and Jacob is the God of the philosophers or not, he will have to admit that

[21] Jacques Maritain, *Introduction to Philosophy*, translated by E. I. Natkins (London, Longmans, Green and Company, 1930), p. 134.
[22] Zuurdeeg, *An Analytical Philosophy of Religion*, p. 19.
[23] *Ibid.*, p. 50.
[24] *Ibid.*, p. 98.
[25] Dawson, p. 44.

the traditional philosophical arguments for God have served to
relate the being taken to be disclosed in the revelatory events to
the general intellectual and scientific culture of the community.
As such, they formed the very heart of natural theology. It is the
purpose of this section to examine some of the traditional philosophical arguments for the existence of God in the light of
some of the tools developed by contemporary logic and linguistic
studies and to determine whether or not these arguments may be
rephrased in such a way that they can perform this meaningful
function today. I shall not, however, be concerned with constructing any theological proofs. Our problem is methodological,
and we shall only raise the question as to how such proofs may
be constructed. First, I shall attempt an informal analysis of St.
Anselm's so-called ontological argument and the first of St. Thomas's Five Ways, in order to determine the nature of the arguments which are being proposed. In the light of this analysis I
shall attempt to reformulate the problem in terms of a more
contemporary methodology.

For our discussion of the ontological argument, let us take
St. Anselm's second formulation of the argument for, as Hartshorne [26] points out, this formulation avoids the thorny problem
of 'existence' being used as a predicate. St. Anselm begins his
discussion by characterizing God as "that than which nothing
greater can be conceived". His argument, itself, may be stated
in four steps:

1. ... it is possible to conceive of a being which cannot be con-
    ceived not to exist.

2. [Such a being] is greater than one which can be conceived
    not to exist.

3. Hence, if that than which nothing greater can be conceived,
    can be conceived not to exist, it is not that than which nothing
    greater can be conceived.

[26]   Hartshorne, *Logic of Perfection*, p. 57.

4. There is then, so truly a being than which nothing greater can be conceived to exist, that it cannot even be conceived not to exist.[27]

In analyzing the proof, it is obvious that the key point around which it revolves is the phrase 'that than which nothing greater can be conceived'. This phrase is certainly not intended to be a definition of God, in the sense of stating his essence. For St. Anselm, in his reply to Gaunilo, leaves open the possibility of the incomprehensibility of the nature of God: "When one says, *that than which nothing greater is conceivable,* undoubtedly what is heard is conceivable and intelligible, although that being itself, than which a greater is inconceivable, cannot be conceived or understood." [28] If this phrase is not taken to be a definition or even a definite description, then what is it? In step 3, above, the saint used this characterization as a criterion of any adequate concept of God. What step 3 seems to say is that the concept of any being which can be conceived not to exist simply is not a conception of God, since any conception of God must meet the criterion of being a conception of that than which nothing greater can be conceived. Let us take the phrase, "that than which nothing greater can be conceived", then as a criterion for any adequate concept of God.

In his proof, St. Anselm also uses the phrase, "the conception of a being". Since, in contemporary linguistic studies, one speaks of definitions or definite descriptions rather than concepts and since here St. Anselm is speaking of *a* being, or an individual, let us interpret his phrase as "a definite description of an individual". Such phrases as "cannot be conceived not to exist" and "can be conceived not to exist" may be interpreted as "necessarily exists" and "does not necessarily exist". St. Anselm, himself, in his reply to Gaunilo [29] uses "whose non-existence is

[27] Anselm, *Proslogium; Monologium, etc.*, translated by S. N. Deane (Lasalle, Open Court, 1958), pp. 8-9.
[28] *Ibid.*, p. 168.
[29] *Ibid.*, p. 169.

impossible" and "whose non-existence is possible" in his re-
statement of this same argument. If we accept these modifica-
tions in the saint's argument, then it may be rephrased as follows:

1a. It is possible to formulate a definite description of an in-
     dividual which necessarily exists.

2a. An individual which necessarily exists is greater than an in-
     dividual which does not necessarily exist.

3a. From step 2a and the criterion for an adequate definite
     description for God, it follows that an adequate definite
     description for God cannot be such that God does not nec-
     essarily exist.

4a. From step 1a and step 2a it follows that God necessarily
     exists.

Of course, the conclusion of step 4a rests upon step 1a; that is,
the possibility of formulating a definite description of an individual which necessarily exists. And this is precisely what St.
Anselm has not shown in his proof. In fact, what St. Anselm has
demonstrated in his proof is that if it is possible to formulate an
adequate definite description for God, then God necessarily
exists. Otherwise, the definite description would not be an adequate definite description of God. As a matter of fact, St. Anselm,
himself, summarizes the argument in precisely this way – allowing
for our change in terminology. He writes in his reply to Gaunilo:
"If such a being can be conceived to exist, necessarily it does
exist." [30] The problem which the ontological argument itself does
not answer is, Can an adequate definite description for God be
formulated?

It would seem that an adequate definite description for God
must meet at least these three conditions: First, it must be a
consistent definite description. Otherwise, the existence of God
would be an impossibility. Secondly, the definite description must
be formulated in terms of predicates which are descriptively

[30] *Ibid.*, p. 154.

meaningful. If not, there would be a question as to whether or not it was a "possible concept". Thirdly, the definite description must be such that the individual described is a necessary, not a contingent individual. This, of course, follows from St. Anselm's third step. The first condition needs no explanation since here we are merely speaking of logical consistency. The second condition, perhaps, needs some clarification and justification, but at the risk of being dogmatic, let us say that by descriptively meaningful predicates we mean only those predicates which are used to describe what we have called the common world disclosed to us in experience. The third condition raises a far more serious problem of interpretation: What is the meaning of 'necessary' in this context? Here St. Anselm gives us a clue in his answer to Gaunilo. In interpreting the phrase, "whose non-existence is possible", he writes: "Whatever at any place or at any time does not exist – even if it does exist at some place or at some time – can be conceived to exist nowhere and never, as at some place and at some time it does not exist." [31] Of a necessary individual, or one whose non-existence is impossible, the saint writes: "By no means, then, does it at any place or at any time fail to exist as a whole: but it exists as a whole everywhere and always." [32] A necessary individual, then, according to St. Anselm, is an omnipresent individual. It is an individual which if any spatio-temporal individual exists, this individual exists. Or alternatively, the existence of this individual is a necessary condition for the existence of any spatio-temporal individual. This is, in a way, an explication of God in terms of the creator of the world. For does not the image of God as creator portray him as a necessary condition for the existence of any spatio-temporal individuals whatever, or for the existence of any possible world? In summary, the problem of an adequate definite description for God becomes the problem of formulating a consistent definite description of an individual in terms of the predicates used to describe the

[31]   *Ibid.*, p. 155.
[32]   *Ibid.*, p. 156.

spatio-temporal individuals given in experience and such that God is a necessary condition for the existence of any spatio-temporal individual. This I take to be precisely the task of the various cosmological arguments for the existence of God. In order to illustrate this, let us examine the first of St. Thomas's Five Ways.

St. Thomas's first argument may be summarized in nine steps as follows:

1. It is certain, and evident to our senses, that in the world some things are in motion.

2. Motion is nothing else than the reduction of something from potentiality to actuality.

3. Nothing can be reduced from potentiality to actuality, except by something in a state of actuality.

4. It is impossible that the same thing should be at once in actuality and potentiality in the same respect.

5. It is therefore impossible that in the same respect and in the same way a thing should be both mover and moved.

6. Therefore, whatever is moved must be moved by another.

7. If that by which it is moved be itself moved, then this also must need be moved by another and that by another.

8. (a) But this cannot go on to infinity, because then there would be no first mover, and consequently, no other mover, seeing (b) that subsequent movers move only in as much as they are moved by the first mover.

9. (a) Therefore, it is necessary to arrive at a first mover, moved by no other, (b) and this everyone understands to be God.[33]

There seem to be three key points in this proof: 1) that "a first mover, moved by no other" is what everyone understands to be

---

[33] Thomas Aquinas, *Summa Theologica*, I, Q. 11, a. 3. All quotations are taken from Anton C. Pegis revision of the English Dominican translation in *Basic Writings of Saint Thomas Aquinas* (New York, Random House, 1945).

God, 9 (b); 2) that an analysis of the properties of the relation, x moves y, demonstrates the necessity of the existence of a first mover, moved by no other, 2-9 (a); and 3) that it is obvious that this relation characterizes the common spatio-temporal world disclosed to us in experience, 1.

The first point, which is step 9 (b) in the proof, gives us what we have called a definite description of God; that is, a characterization which is applicable to one and only one individual. The third point, or step 1 in the proof, assures us that the two place predicate, 'x moves y', is a meaningful descriptive predicate for it does, in fact, characterize the common world disclosed in experience. This assures us that the field of the relation is not empty. In fact, it is motion in this general sense, or change, which distinguishes what we mean by the spatio-temporal world from the non-spatio-temporal, or eternal. The second point is the heart of St. Thomas's proof. In 2-9 (a) he attempts to demonstrate that the properties of the relation, x moves y, necessitate a first unmoved mover. If his proof is successful, then the existence of God is a necessary condition for the existence of any moving individual.

Step 5 asserts that the relation is irreflexive; that is, $(x) \sim xMx$. Steps 2-4 are an attempt to demonstrate that this follows from what, in this context, is meant by motion, or change; that is, a reduction from potentiality to actuality. That this is St. Thomas's intention is indicated by him when, in the *Summa Contra Gentiles,* he considers the denial of step 5, which he attributes to Plato. The saint writes:

It is to be noted, however, that Plato, who held that every mover is moved (*Phaedrus* 247C), understood the name motion in a wider sense than did Aristotle. . . . According to Plato, however, that which moves itself is not a body. Plato understood by motion any given operation, so that to understand and to judge are a kind of motion.[34]

[34]   Thomas Aquinas, *Summa Contra Gentiles,* I, Ch. 13, 10. All quotations from the *Summa* are taken from the Anton C. Pegis translation, *On the Truth of the Catholic Faith* (New York, Doubleday and Company, Inc., 1955).

Thus, St. Thomas himself takes a denial of step 5 to be a disagreement over the meaning of the "name motion", rather than a disagreement which could be settled on the basis of observation.

Steps 6 seems to follow from a definition of 'x is moved' (MDx); that is, $(\exists y)yMx$ and step 5, $(x)\sim xMx$, so that we have $(x)[MDx \equiv (\exists y)(yMx \cdot \sim x=y)]$. And from this step 7 follows. Step 8 is more complex. Step 8 (b) asserts that the relation, x moves y, is a transitive ordering relation, while 8 (a) seems to assert that any linear series ordered by the relation, x moves y, has an initial member, therefore, the whole set ordered by the relation, x moves y, has an initial member which is moved by no other. If this is what the saint is arguing, then it bears a striking resemblance to Zorn's Lemma. The statement of this point in the *Summa Contra Gentiles* is even clearer:

In an ordered series of movers and things moved (this is a series in which one is moved by another according to an order), it is necessarily the fact that, when the first mover is removed or ceases to move, no other mover will be moved. For the first mover is the cause of motion for all the others. But, if there are movers and things moved following an order to infinity, there would be no first mover, but all would be as intermediate movers. Therefore, none of the others will be able to be moved, and thus nothing in the world will be moved.[35]

Whether this interpretation of the saint is right or not, it is obvious that the question of an infinite series of movers and things moved is not one that can be settled on the basis of observation. Like irreflexsivity and transitivity, it is a question of what properties characterize the relation, x moves y. In other words, it is a question either of the definition of the two place predicate, 'x moves y', or a question, if the predicate is taken as primitive, of what axioms govern this two place predicate.

I think a similar analysis can be done for the other four of St. Thomas's Five Ways. In each he proposes a definite description for God in terms of certain general relations which were used to characterize the sensible world. For the general characteristics

[35] *Ibid.*, I, Ch. 13, 14.

of efficient causality, he proposes the first efficient cause; for contingency, the non-contingent, or necessary individual; for gradations of value, the cause of all value; and for rational order, the intelligent cause of all rational order. And his arguments are attempts to demonstrate that these general characteristics logically necessitate the existence of this individual. As Professor Harrison has put it,

It follows, for Aquinas, that someone is involved in a contradiction if he affirms the statements "there are things which change" and "there are things which come into being and pass away", and at the same time denies the statements "there is a supreme unmoved mover" and "there is an absolutely necessary being".[36]

In no case, then, do the conclusions rest upon the existence of any particular individuals in the sensible world; they rest solely upon the fact that there is a sensible world at all. Consequently, the truth or falsity of the statement. 'God exists', is for St. Thomas independent of the truth or falsity of any statement about the existence of any contingent individual whatever. To quote Professor Harrison again, ". . . the proofs do not require the discovery of any new empirical data, which the method of the natural sciences would call for." [37] On the contrary, the statement asserting the existence of God follows solely from the axioms which were used to characterize the common world disclosed in experience. As was suggested earlier, this should be no surprise; for after all, one of the main notions involved in the concept of God is that of the creator of the world. Consequently, it should be irrelevant exactly what individuals make up the world; God would still exist as creator. Therefore, the existence of no particular individual creature included in what we call the world could count either for or against the existence of the creator. In other words, any statement asserting either the existence or non-existence of an individual should logically imply the state-

[36] F. R. Harrison, "Some Brief Remarks Concerning the *Quinque Viae* of Saint Thomas", *Franciscan Studies*, XXI (1961), p. 85.
[37] *Ibid.*, p. 80.

ment asserting the existence of God. This seems to be exactly what St. Anselm's ontological argument requires.

In terms of what we have called a descriptive language adequate for describing the common world disclosed to us in experience and in light of our analysis of the traditional arguments for the existence of God, it seems that the theological problem becomes the problem of constructing an adequate definite description for God in terms of our primitive symbols and demonstrating that the statement asserting his existence is necessarily true – that is, that the statement follows from the rules of the language. As such, the statement asserting God's existence would be logically implied by any contingent statement whatever. If such a task is possible, this would assure us both of the necessary character and of the descriptive character of the statement, 'There is a God'. An additional problem for natural theology, of course, would be to define in terms of a descriptive linguistic framework the traditional attributes of God and demonstrate that they follow the definite description.

D. LANGUAGE AND REVEALED THEOLOGY

In order that we may turn to the problem of revealed theology, let us assume that the natural theologian has been able to perform his task and has provided us with a descriptively meaningful definite description for the name, 'God', and a set of necessary statements about him. The purpose of the theologian's task, as we outlined it, was to specify descriptively that being who was taken to be disclosed in the revelatory events. We must now turn to the problem of the language used in recording these events and its relation to doctrines traditionally considered as revealed and to raise the question of the descriptive character of these doctrines.

In order to determine the nature of the statements which traditionally have belonged to revealed theology and their relation to the record of revelation, let us follow again a clue given by St. Thomas Aquinas. In his *Summa Theologica,* St. Thomas writes:

The author of Holy Scripture is God in whose power it is to signify His meanings, not by words only (as a man can do), but also by things themselves. So, whereas in every other science things are signified by words, this science has the property that the things signified by the words have themselves also a signification ... that first signification whereby words signify things belongs to the first sense, the historical or literal. That signification whereby things signified by words have themselves also a signification is called the spiritual sense, which is based on the literal, and presupposes it.[38]

In this quote St. Thomas is suggesting that there is within the domain of revealed theology a set of statements about things in the common world disclosed to us in experience and that these statements are to be taken as any historical statement. This is their literal sense. This group of statements corresponds to what we called the record of revelation. If these statements are to be taken as historical statements, then they must be taken as descriptive statements and their truth value must be determined in the same manner as any historical statement. It is not, however, their truth or falsity which makes these statements a part of revealed theology. As true historical statements, if they are in fact true, they belong to history. What places them within the domain of revealed theology is that the things described in these statements are also taken as having a signification, and it is this signification of the things described in the record that is the spiritual signification. For revealed theology, however, the truth or falsity of these statements is irrelevant. For we must allow for what Dante has called "beauteous fiction" [39] and H. W. Robinson, more appropriately, the "ministry of illusion".[40] Let us take,

---

[38]   Thomas Aquinas, *Summa Theologica,* I. Q. 1, a. 10.
[39]   Dante, "First Treatise", *The Convivo,* editor P. H. Wickstead (London, J. M. Dent and Sons, 1940), p. 63 (1.25).
[40]   H. W. Robinson, *Inspiration and Revelation in the Old Testament* (Oxford, Clarendon Press, 1946), p. 45.

for example, the statement, 'Jesus of Nazareth was crucified under Pontius Pilot'. This statement, as such, is a descriptive statement and obeys the rules of descriptive statements and its truth value must be determined in the same manner as the truth value of any other descriptive statement in history. But what places this statement in the domain of revealed theology is that the thing described by the statement has itself a signification.

In order to clarify how things, as well as words, can have a signification, let us see how things themselves can function as signs. The emphasis in contemporary philosophy on the use of linguistic signs tends to blind us to the fact that most of our signs are not linguistic signs. Suppose, for example, that as you walked out the door this morning, you looked up at the sky and saw a black cloud. And you then returned to your room, got your umbrella and raincoat. What would you have done? You would have been taking the black cloud as a sign of rain; for you it signified rain. And you interpreted this sign in terms of a certain type of behavior – your returning and getting your umbrella and raincoat. Not a single linguistic sign entered into this chain of events. On the other hand, suppose that you, upon seeing the black cloud, uttered this prediction: 'It is going to rain'. This would be an interpretation in terms of a verbal prediction. But in either case, the black cloud signified you for rain and served as a promise, a promise of rain.

Now let us return to St. Thomas and see how the things described in the record of revelation signify. He continues:

... so far as the things of the Old Law signify the things of the new law, there is the allegorical sense; so far as the things done in Christ, or so far as the things which signify Christ, are signs of what we ought to do, there is the moral sense. But so far as they signify what relates to eternal glory, there is the anagogical sense.[41]

In this quote St. Thomas has listed three ways in which the events described in the record of revelation may have spiritual

[41]   Thomas Aquinas, *Summa Theologica*, I, Q. 1, a. 10.

significance. First, there is what he calls the allegorical sense. The word 'allegory' comes from two Greek words, 'to speak' and 'another'. To give an allegory is literally to speak of another. Here the things of the Old Testament are taken as signifying, or speaking of, the things of the New Testament. The previous illustration of the black cloud as a sign will, I think, be helpful here. Just as the black cloud served as a promise of rain, so the things of the Old Testament are interpreted as promises of things to come in the New Testament. That this type of interpretation is not foreign to the Bible itself goes without saying. It is this pattern of promise and fulfillment which gives the Biblical narrative the dramatic continuity of which we spoke. The application of the term, 'Messiah', or its Greek cognate, 'Christ', to Jesus of Nazareth is the affirmation that in him the promises of the Old Testament are fulfilled. In fact, what appears to be the earliest affirmation of the Christian Church is: "Let all the house of Israel therefore know assuredly that God has made him both Lord and Christ, this Jesus whom you crucified" (*R. S. V.*, Acts 2 : 36).

Secondly, there is what St. Thomas has called the moral sense of signification. Here the behavior of Jesus of Nazareth and the things which signify him are taken as signs of how we ourselves should behave. This is to give expression to Jesus' exhortation: "If any man will come after me let him take up his cross and follow me" (*R. S. V.*, Matthew 16 : 24). Thirdly, there is what St. Thomas has called the anagogical sense. The word 'anagogical' comes from the Greek verb, 'to raise up'. Dante interprets the use of the word, 'anagogical', in this context as meaning "above the sense".[42] Here the things of the sensible world are taken as signifying not some future things in the world of sense, as the allegorical, nor are they taken as signifying how we should act in this life, as the moral, but as signifying our eternal glory – that is, signifying something about God.

In the illustration which used the black cloud as a sign, it was

[42] Dante, p. 64 (1.52).

suggested that a sign may be interpreted either in terms of a certain type of behavior or in the form of a verbal prediction. Let us say that the behavioral interpretation of the signs of revelation constitute the Christian life. Herein lies the efficacy of the revelatory events. Since, however, we are concerned with religious language, it is the verbal interpretations which interest us. To give a verbal interpretation of the signs which are taken as promises is to prophesy. This is what Plato, in the *Phaedrus,* calls the first type of divine madness. To give a verbal interpretation of the signs in the moral sense is to exhort, or to give moral imperatives. To give a verbal interpretation of the signs in an anagogical sense is to give the doctrines of revealed theology.

Neither the prophecies nor the exhortations are statements; for these verbal expressions do not function descriptively. I would like to maintain, however, that the anagogical verbal interpretations, which I take to be the revealed doctrines, do function descriptively; that is, they are taken as statements describing something about God. Now if this is the case, this means that we must be able to say what kind of truth conditions are to be given for these doctrines.

E. THE PROBLEM OF TRUTH CONDITIONS

In order to clarify this point let us once again return to the use of the black cloud as a sign. Granted that neither your behavioral interpretation, nor your verbal interpretation of the black cloud in the form of a prediction is a statement, still one can raise the question as to whether or not your interpretation is justified. If you interpreted the black cloud as a sign of rain, the thing that would justify your interpretation would be the fact of rain – in other words, the fulfillment of the promise. And the verbal expression which states the fact which fulfills the promise should be a statement which is either true or false. If this were not the case, then one interpretation would be as justifiable as another and we would have no way of distinguishing the false prophet from the true prophet. We maintained that it was the Christian affirmation that the promises of the Old Testament were fulfilled in Jesus of Nazareth and the verbal expression which justifies these interpretations is: 'Jesus is the Christ, or Messiah'.

Likewise, even though exhortations are not statements, we can raise the question of their justification. The Christian is exhorted to "take up his cross and follow" because Jesus is Lord. But Jesus' lordship finds its justification in his messiahship. And here again our justification for the moral interpretation rests upon the messianic office of Jesus. We must, then, raise the question whether or not the verbal expression, 'Jesus of Nazareth is the Messiah' is a statement. The only basis upon which the allegorical and the moral interpretations can be justified is that this verbal expression is a statement and is true. But if it is a statement, then truth conditions must be given for it. These truth conditions cannot be given in terms of Jesus of Nazareth's meeting the stipulations in the promises, for it is he who determines which prophecies are justified and which are not. That is, he, in the end, is used to distinguish the false prophet from the true prophet. Likewise the truth conditions cannot be given in terms of his meeting certain moral requirements, for it is he who justifies the moral exhortations of the Christian.

If Jesus of Nazareth is in fact the Messiah, then he has this office solely on the basis of God's approval. In the end, the crux of the Christian revelation rests upon the reported voice which came from heaven upon the baptism of Jesus: "This is my beloved Son, with whom I am well pleased" (R. S. V., Matthew 3 : 17). In other words, the truth conditions for the statement, 'Jesus is the Messiah', must ultimately be given in terms of God's approval of him for this role. To quote again from Peter's sermon in Acts, ". . . God has made him both Lord and Christ". In fact, I would like to propose that all revealed doctrines, in so far as they are descriptive sentences, assert something about God's approvals and disapprovals, or his evaluations of the things of this world, and that their truth conditions must in the end be given in these terms. It is precisely because of this fact that they can be said to be revelations of the character of God. Is it not a person's approvals and disapprovals, or his evaluations, that reveal his character? So it is with God. It is for this reason that God's judgment plays an essential role in the Biblical revelation. The Divine Yes and the Divine No reveal the character of God. And it is these statements which give us what St. Thomas has called the anagogical interpretations of the things recorded in Scripture. Here the things are taken as signs of God's evaluations and thus a revelation of his character. And the revealed doctrines are true in so far as they state what are, in fact, God's evaluations and false in so far as they do not.

Throughout this analysis of revealed theology we have, of course, assumed that the natural theologian has succeeded in his task and given us a descriptive meaning for the term, 'God'. Likewise, we have assumed that he has been able to define the various traditional attributes of omnipresence, omniscience, omnipotence, and goodness, or perfection. But if we are to give meaning to the verbal expressions of revealed theology, then the natural theologian must also be able to give descriptive meaning to the notion of God's evaluation of the world. In other words, he must be able, in terms of God's goodness, or perfection, to give a definition for the expression, 'x is more valuable to God than y'. Of course, if the task of natural theology is an impossible task, then the verbal expressions of revealed theology, as well as the verbal expressions of natural theology, become questionable. In this way revelation is dependent upon natural theology – that is, for its meaningfulness. There are good indications, however, that the task of natural theology is not an impossible one.

For the purposes of our discussion, however, let us assume once again that this task has been accomplished. It seems obvious that a statement of the form, 'x is more valuable to God than y', cannot be determined to be either true or false on the basis of human observation. At least it is not at all clear what sort of observations are called for. Also, a statement of the form, 'x is more valuable to God than y', could not be shown to be necessarily true; that is, we could not determine its truth value by appealing to our rules and axioms. This can be indicated by comparing a statement of this form, to a statement of the form, 'God knows x'. Now if omniscience has been defined, then to be known by God would be a universal property of all individuals. In fact, this is precisely what omniscience means. Consequently, a statement of the form, 'God knows x', no matter what x might be, would be necessarily true. On the other hand, to be more valuable to God than something else could not possibly be a universal property and, consequently, could not be proven of any individual. This means, then, that to accept as true any statement concerning God's evaluations of the world is to entertain a non-verifiable belief, for it seems to be technologically beyond the power of human beings to determine by any methodology whether or not its truth conditions do in fact hold.

Thus is seems that we are left with a set of beliefs, those beliefs about God's evaluations of the world, which cannot be justified by any methodology. Yet these beliefs, it would seem, should determine to a large extent our attitude toward life and the world and have serious consequences for our actions. But these are beliefs which can only be accepted or rejected on the basis of faith. The status of theological beliefs suggested here is perhaps best expressed by Socrates in his closing remarks to the judges who had just voted to condemn him to death:

The hour of departure has arrived, and we go our ways – I to die, and you to live. Which is better God only knows.

But I hasten to add: If God does know then that makes a difference, for it makes revealed theology possible. But the problem of whether or not it makes sense to say 'God knows' depends upon the possibility of natural theology and metaphysics, the problem to which we must now turn.

V

AN EXPLICATION OF THE TERM 'GOD' FOR NATURAL THEOLOGY

In speaking of the term 'God', Peirce writes, " 'God' is a vernacular word and, like all such words, but more than almost any, is vague." [1] I think there are very few who would disagree with Peirce on this point; however, I must disagree with Peirce that this particular vernacular word, with its vagueness, answers "the principle purposes". For a clear and precise definite description of God is basic to any discussion of theological language and the first task of natural theology. At the very beginning of the *Summa Theologica*, St. Thomas, for example, in his Five Ways offers proofs for the existence of a 'First Cause', an 'Unmoved Mover', etc., and at the end of each proof he adds a clause such as, 'and this everyone understands to be God'. Thus, he offers a more precise concept, for example, First Cause, as a substitute for the vague concept God. Carnap has given the name 'explication' to this procedure whereby "a new precisely defined concept is introduced in place of one which is familiar but insufficiently precise".[2] This new concept he calls the *explicatum*. The first task of natural theology is to construct an adequate explicatum for 'God' in its ordinary meaning, or in one of its meanings if there are several. This chapter will be concerned with formulating only an informal explicatum, one that can serve as a basis for a formal explicatum in a formal metaphysical language. Also, since our concern is with natural theology, we shall be concerned with only the general aspects of God – that is, God as he is related to any and every event.

---

[1]   C. S. Peirce, *Collected Papers*, VI, 494.
[2]   Rudolf Carnap, *Introduction to Symbolic Logic*, translated by William H. Meyer and John Wilkinson (New York, Dover Publ., Inc., 1958), p. 2.

A. THE PROBLEM OF EXPLICATING 'GOD'

In *Existence and Analogy,* Mascall tells us that the Christian knows what he means by 'God' because "the Bible and the Church have told him". He has only to "institute a purely rational inquiry into the grounds for asserting that God exists".[3] There is some doubt as to whether the problem is quite so simple, even for the traditional Christian. Certainly for an explicatum for 'God' in natural theology, one cannot rely solely on what "the Bible and the Church have told him". What he must seek to formulate, in so far as it is possible, is a precise explicatum which expresses what most people seem to have in mind when they use the word 'God'. This is not a question of Biblical or ecclesiastical authority, but a question of common usage. And this is no easy task.

In addition to the vagueness and ambiguity in the concept of God as we find it in common religious usage, there is an additional difficulty. It is the difficulty of the extra-religious use of the concept, particularly in the philosophical traditions. In addition to the role which 'God' has played in religious devotion, ritual, practice, and belief, it has played an equally prominent role in philosophy. In fact, its role in philosophy is as old as philosophy itself. Its use goes back to the traditional father of philosophy, Thales, who used the principle, "all things are full of gods",[4] to explain aspects of the universe. And it was Aristotle [5] who first suggested a science of theology as a part of philosophy. Even in these early beginnings, however, to say nothing of later developments in philosophy, one is at times hard pressed to find much in common between the role which the concept plays in religious devotion and the role it plays in philosophy.[6]

[3]   E. L. Mascall, *Existence and Analogy*, p. 17.
[4]   Aristotle, *De Anima*, 411a, 7. All quotations from Aristotle are from *The Basic Works of Aristotle*, edited by Richard McKeon (New York, Random House, 1941).
[5]   Aristotle, *Metaphysics*, 1026a, 19 and 1064b, p. 3.
[6]   John Burnet, *Early Greek Philosophy* (London, A. C. Black, 1930), pp. 14-15.

In explicating the term 'God', one must begin, however, with the concept as it is found in religion, not in philosophy. For as Hartshorne has rightly pointed out, "religion seems clearly to have first title to the word".[7] Wherever the term 'God' has appeared in philosophy, it has been taken over from religion because it, in some of its aspects, was found to be philosophically useful, or philosophy felt called upon to take into account religious experience. Thus in order to give what might be considered an adequate explication of the concept of a God, one need not be as ambitious as St. Thomas and assert of his explicatum, "this everyone understands to be God". He need only be able to say of his explicatum, "this religious men in general understand to be God".

Granted the need of an explication of the concept of God and given the great diversity of religious belief and practice, the question immediately arises: How do we begin an explication? In *He Who Is,* Mascall tells us that St. Thomas sees

God's fundamental attribute as that of self-subsistent being. . . . And the conception of God as *ipsum esse subsistents*, is fundamental to his whole discussion of the divine nature. It draws into a unity all the other attributes and operations of God. . . .[8]

This quotation gives us a pattern for an explication. One must begin by seeking some one fundamental attribute or aspect of God which "draws into a unity all the other attributes and operations of God". For in some sense, as Tillich observes, "the classical doctrine that the divine attributes are identical is correct".[9] Or as Hartshorne has put it,

We speak of a variety of properties, the usual attributes, but they turn out to be merely different ways of conceiving one unique property.

[7]   Charles Hartshorne, *Man's Vision of God* (New York, Harper and Brothers, 1948), p. 98.
[8]   E. L. Mascal, *He Who Is* (New York, Longmans, Green and Company, 1948), p. 13.
[9]   Paul Tillich, *Systematic Theology*, I, 11.

Omniscience and omnipotence are not related like having hoofs and having horns.[10]

The problem of explication, then, is the problem of finding this "one fundamental attribute" or "one unique property".

Ironically, the key to that "one fundamental attribute" which can serve as the beginning of a religious explication of God and the cornerstone of natural theology can be found in the work which is frequently hailed as the death knell of natural theology, *The Dialogues Concerning Natural Religion*. In Part II, Hume has Philo say in reply to Demea, God "is more the object of worship in the temple, than of disputation in the schools".[11] Although one may disagree with Philo and think that God can be at home in the schools as well as in the temple, he must agree that whatever men may think God to be, he is primarily "an object of worship". If we take seriously the etymology of the English word 'worship', we can derive that "one unique property" which we need for an explication. The word 'worship' is derived from two Anglo-Saxon words: 'weorth' (worth) and 'scipe' (ship), a suffix denoting something exhibiting, or embodying, a quality or state. Thus, an object of worship is something embodying the quality of superior worth, or value. Whatever else people may have in mind when they use the terms 'gods' and 'God', they are at least referring to beings of superior value, or to one being of supreme value.

As Mascall has pointed out,[12] theologians have taken many different attributes as primary: Aristotle took thought, and St. Augustine took subsistent Truth as primary. It can be said that Duns Scotus took infinity and, as it is frequently maintained, St. Thomas took subsistent being. All of these, however, are primarily philosophical, not religious, attributes. No matter how respected these traditions may be, Hartshorne is right:

---

[10]   Hartshorne, p. 321.
[11]   David Hume, *Dialogues Concerning Natural Religion* (New York, Hafner, 1957), p. 16.
[12]   Mascall, p. 10.

... the rational way ... is first to allow religion to assert what its claims are, and to avoid the error of supposing that these claims can only be such as are statable in terms of a given, say Neo-Platonic or Aristotelian, philosophy.[13]

Thus, if we take the religious role as primary, we must take the property of being of supreme value as the fundamental one which will form the basis of the explication.

This, of course, is not a novel idea. "And, indeed", wrote St. Anselm, "we believe that thou art a being than which no greater can be conceived".[14] Kierkegaard saw God primarily as the object of "infinite passion and interest", and Tillich sees him as "our ultimate concern". These are all expressions of the same fundamental idea which Garnett summarizes as "something other than the self which is regarded as worthy of supreme devotion".[15] It is this concept of beings of superior value (gods), or of a being of supreme value (God) which seems basic to religion, and it is this which religious men in general understand to be God. Any role which the concept of God plays in philosophy must, in some sense, be derivative from this primary religious notion. As Tillich writes:

Whether it is "being-itself" (Scholastics) or the "universal substance" (Spinoza), whether it is "beyond objectivity and subjectivity" (James) or the "identity of spirit and nature" (Schelling), whether it is "universe" (Schleiermacher) or "cosmic whole" (Hocking), whether it is "value creating process" (Whitehead) or "progressive integration" (Weiman), whether it is "absolute spirit" (Hegel) or "cosmic person" (Brightman) – each of these concepts is based on an immediate experience of someting ultimate in value....[16]

The problem of explicating the concept of God for natural theology, then, may be interpreted as the task of formulating a precise and adequate definite description of a being who can be considered as supremely valuable; and the problem of theological

---

[13]   Hartshorne, p. x.
[14]   St. Anselm, *Proslogium, Monologium, etc.*, p. 7.
[15]   A. C. Garnett, *Religion and the Moral Life* (New York, Ronald Press, 1955), p. 6.
[16]   Tillich, I, 9.

proofs is, as we suggested earlier, the problem of demonstrating that the traditional notions of omnipotence, omniscience, omnipresence, necessary existence, etc. are contained in it.

B. AN EXPLICATUM

In his *Systematic Theology*, Tillich [17] suggests that his conception of God as the "ultimate concern" is only an abstract translation of the great commandment: "The Lord, your God, the Lord is one; and you shall love the Lord your God with all your heart, and with all your soul and with all your mind, and with all your strength" (Mark 12 : 29, 30, R.S.V.). Can we formulate a definite description for such a being? If we mean by this, can we give a traditional definition in terms of genus and species, then Gilson is right: "In the case of God all definition is impossible." [18] For God as the supreme object of worship is unique and has no rival. There can be only one being who can merit the love of *all* our heart, soul, mind, and strength. Also, if we seek a detailed description of God in all his concreteness, our task is hopeless. It is this fact that has given rise to the notion that we cannot know the essence of God and to the popularity of negative theology. For example, Gilson writes:

... it is impossible for us to conceive of a perfect being, but we must affirm God to be such, denying Him all imperfection. Moreover, this is what we do in affirming that God is perfect.... To make God known by way of negation .... [19]

Such a purely negative approach recommends itself, however, only upon the condition that there is no positive content whatsoever in the concept of a supremely valuable being. A content may be found if we ask what would be the conditions which a being

---

[17] *Ibid.*, I, 11.
[18] Etienne Gilson, *The Christian Philosophy of St. Thomas Aquinas*, translated by L. K. Shook (London, V. Gollancz, 1957), p. 96.
[19] *Ibid.*, p. 97.

would have to fulfill in order to merit the love of all our heart, all our soul, and all our mind, and all our strength?

It would seem that the best candidate for the supremely valuable being would be a being who is the necessary condition for any value whatsoever. This being would be the ground of all value, and the negation of his existence would be the negation of all value, possible or actual. And if we accept the notion, which most religious traditions do, that existence itself is valuable – that is, it is better for anything to exist than not to exist – then the negation of his existence would be the negation of all existence. Such a being would surely be placed above all else in the scale of value, and this seems to be what lies behind the classical deification of the First Cause.

Is this, however, an adequate conception of a being who can command the love of *all* our heart, soul, mind, and strength, that is, our total devotion? Or, can we conceive of another more worthy? This notion of a First Cause can be seen to be inadequate if we place along side the first commandment, the second: "You shall love your neighbor as yourself" (Mark 12 : 31, R.S.V.). Have we not been commanded to love something other than God and, thus, to divide our devotion? There is something now more worthy of our total devotion, namely, the "necessary condition for all value" *and* the "totality of all actual value" including our neighbor, ourselves, and anything else of value. We have only one alternative: to place, in some sense, all that is valuable in the creature in God, so that when we love God with *all* our heart, we, at the same time, love all that is valuable in the creatures. Gilson can say of God, "To love his creatures is for God but to love Himself. . . . Thus God loves all in loving Himself." [20] The same must be said for man: To love God is to love the creature in him. In this sense the gospel writer is right: the second commandment is "like" the first.

We can now characterize God as the being who is a necessary condition for all value and who includes within himself all actual

20   *Ibid.*, p. 118.

value. Both of these notions seem essential to our explicatum for 'God'. The first notion places God above all other beings which may be of value; he is in a unique category. They are all dependent upon him for their existence, but he, in turn, is not dependent upon them for his existence. The second assures him undivided devotion. There is nothing "outside" him. This seems to be what Ramsey is attempting to express with his analogy of a mathematical sequence beginning with one and proceeding such that each time there is added half of what was added the previous time so that the sequence continues to approach two. Two, however, is not in the sequence and has "a different logical status ... from the terms of the series".[21] It lies outside the series, determining the sequence and including the sequence.

Both of these notions, being a necessary condition for all possible value and including all actual value, can even be illustrated with the humanistic thesis. These same notions lie behind the humanist's feeling when he finds his "supremely worthy object of devotion in human society".[22] Since he limits all possible and actual value to human value – a rather questionable anthropocentric assumption – he is forced to see humanity both as the necessary condition for all possible value and as including all actual value. Thus, humanity becomes for him the supreme object of undivided devotion. If, however, the humanist were to admit the possibility of value beyond human experience, humanity could no longer be the object of his undivided loyalty.

Let us see if we cannot make our explication for 'God' clearer by further explicating these two primary notions. What the first notion of a necessary condition for all possible value seems to express is the statement: 'If the statement "There is a God" is false, then the statement "There is something such that ———" is false'. This is obviously not an empirical statement. The truth of the statement is not determined by observation, but by the rules of the object language in which the two statements in double quotation marks are formulated. Here we have the possibility

21 Ian T. Ramsey, *Religious Language*, p. 69.
22 Garnett, p. 9.

of expressing the notion of a necessary being in a metaphysical object language.

How can a definite description for God be formulated in a metaphysical object language such that the statement 'There is God' has the property of being implied by any existential statement in the language? This may be done by defining 'God' as 'the totality of all possible values', or to use the more traditional phrases, 'the totality of all positive predicates, or perfections'. There is, however, an inherent ambiguity in this phrase, 'the totality of all possible values'. It may be taken as the totality of all values as merely possible, or the totality of all values as actual, or both, and these are frequently confused.[23] The first expresses that aspect of God which is necessarily implied by each existing concrete entity, and as such, it is abstract. And it is the only aspect which is involved in the notion of a necessary condition for all possible value. To say that God is the totality of all value as possible – that is, the abstract condition for anything of value – in no way implies that he is the totality of all value as actual. One of the most important contributions which the use of formal languages can make to natural theology is to make this distinction clear.

If this is true, it is easy to see why the second notion of the inclusion of all actual value is necessary. While the first notion gives us the abstract aspect of God, the second gives us the concrete aspect. Whereas the first notion required an explication in terms of the properties of the metaphysical object language, the second requires what might be called an 'empirical explication'. How can we give any meaning to the notion of including all actual value except by pointing to an example of 'inclusion of value' in experience. How do we include actual things of value except through a sensitivity to them, a sympathetic feeling for and with them. Take, for example, another human being; we include him in so far as his actual joys, loves, and even sufferings

---

[23]   For a historical treatment of this problem see Charles Hartshorne and William L. Reese, *Philosophers Speak of God* (Chicago, University of Chicago Press, 1953).

become our joys, loves, and sufferings through a sensitivity for him. Thus, we include things in ourselves to the degree to which we are sensitive to them. If not the essence of love, is this not a necessary constituent of love? If God is to include all actual value, he must be universally and perfectly sensitive to all creatures. Through God's perfect and universal love all things are included in him. This is the only way of saving our second notion of inclusion from being vacuous.

Thus, we have an informal explicatum for 'God' – a 'being who is a necessary condition for any creature and who through his universal and perfect sensitivity includes all creatures in his experience'. The first notion gives us what Whitehead calls God's primordial nature, and the second what he calls his consequent nature.[24] Given this explicatum, there are two radical differences between God and his creatures. First, God in his abstract nature is not dependent upon any particular creature, yet all creatures are dependent upon him for their existence. Secondly, the creatures in their sensitivity are limited in degree, scope and time, but God in his concrete nature has no limitations upon his sensitivity, neither limitations of degree, scope nor time. Only such a being could merit the love of *all* our heart, soul, mind, and strength. And only of such a being is it safe to say that "this religious men in general understand to be God". For only beside him does all else fade into nothingness. We must now see if the traditional attributes of God are contained witthin this explicatum.

C. THE PROBLEM OF OMNISCIENCE AND TIME

Let us look first at the attribute of omniscience. If a being of supreme value must include all value, possible and actual, in his being and experience, he must be uniquely sensitive to all things

[24] See particularly A. N. Whitehead, *Process and Reality* (New York, The Humanities Press, 1955), Part V, Chapter II.

possible and actual. Is this not omniscience? As Hartshorne writes,

Could we define all actuality, or all possibility, in any other way than as the content of experience as it would be if all vagueness or un-consciousness of reference were overcome with full and clear aware-ness.[25]

What Aristotle affirmed of the soul – "the soul is in a sense all things" – can even more truly be affirmed of God as he has been explicated.

There are at least two problems, however, which arise when one considers God's omniscience in relation to temporal duration and supersession. The first involves the relation of God's omnis-cience to the future, which is not yet. Hartshorne, for example, writes, "knowledge is true if, and only if, it corresponds to reality, and things that have not happened are, in so far, perhaps, not real. To know them would be to know falsely, for there is nothing of the sort of know." [26] On the other hand, if God did not know the future, how could he be omniscient? The second problem concerns the relation of the necessity of God's knowledge to the contingency of things known. How can God's knowledge of contingent things itself be necessary if the things known are truly contingent? Lequier, for example, maintains that this is equivalent to saying "that a thing will be, and that it well might not be".[27] This appears to be a modal contradiction. Both of these problems were pointed to by St. Thomas in the *Summa Contra Gentiles*. Concerning the first difficulty, that singular things do not always exist to be known, he proposes the following dilemma: "either they will be known by God always, or they will be known at some time and not at another".[28] The first alternative is con-sidered by the saint to be impossible "since of that which does not exist, there can be no knowledge. Knowledge deals with what

---

[25] Hartshorne, p. 322.
[26] *Ibid.*, p. 98.
[27] Jules Lequier, *La Recherche d'une Première Vérité*, edited by Renou-vier (Paris, Librairie Armand Colin, 1924), p. 147.
[28] Thomas Aquinas, *Summa Contra Gentiles*, I, Ch. 63, p. 3.

is true, and what does not exist cannot be true".[29] But if one accepts the classical view of God – that is, that the divine intellect is absolutely unchangeable – then the second alternative, that singulars will be known at some time and not at another, is equally impossible.

The second difficulty, the problem of modality, is posed by the Angelic Doctor in this way: First he recognizes that not all singulars come to be of necessity, but that some happen contingently. Now since certain knowledge is knowledge which cannot be deceived, there can be certain knowledge of contingents only when they exist. "But", writes the saint, "all knowledge of the contingent can be deceived when the contingent is future, since the opposite of what is held by knowledge can happen, for if it could not happen, it would then be necessary." [30] Thus it seems to follow that God's knowledge cannot be certain and necessary and at the same time be of contingent things, which may or may not be.

St. Thomas' answers to these two difficulties are crucial, for they lead us to the heart of what I consider to be the major difficulty in the classical conception of God. The problem of God's knowledge of the future, or things which do not always exist, St. Thomas treats in the following manner:

Something can be present to what is eternal only by being present to the whole of it, since the eternal does not have duration of succession. The divine intellect, therefore, sees in the whole of its eternity, as being present to it, whatever takes place through the whole course of time. An yet what takes places in a certain part of time was not always existent.[31]

And again, in the *Summa Theologica* he explains,

His knowledge is measured by eternity, as is also His being; and eternity, being simultaneously whole, comprises all time.... Hence, all things that are in time are present to God from eternity, not only because He has the essence of things present within Him, as some

[29] *Ibid.*, I, Ch. 63, p. 3.
[30] *Ibid.*, I, Ch. 63, p. 4.
[31] *Ibid.*, I, Ch. 66, p. 7.

say, but because His glance is carried from eternity over all things as they are in their presentiality.[32]

The saint goes on to propose as an analogy the relation of the center of a circle to the circumference as a means of clarifying this relationship. As the center of a circle, which is no part of the circumference, is directly opposed to any determinate point on the circumference, so God is equally present to each duration of succession in time.

In discussing the second, or the modal difficulty, St. Thomas seems to draw a distinction between God's knowledge and the object of his knowledge. He tells us, for example, in the *Summa Contra Gentiles*, that "the contingent is opposed to the certitude of knowledge only so far as it is future, not as far as it is present" and "all knowledge, therefore, that bears on something contingent as present can be certain".[33] Here St. Thomas seems to be pointing to a distinction which von Wright has explicated in terms of alethic modality *de re* and epistemic modality *de re*. The alethic modalities are said to be *de re* "when they are about the mode or way in which an individual thing has or has not a certain property".[34] And the epistemic modalities are said to be *de re* "when they are about the mode or way in which an individual thing is known to possess or lack a certain property".[35] St. Thomas has pointed to an instance of this distinction. If something red is present to us, even though the entity has the property red contingently (alethic modality *de re*) we can know it to have the property with certainty or necessarily (epistemic modality *de re*). One concerns the mode in which the thing *has* the property and the other concerns the mode in which one *knows* the thing to have the property. In the light of this distinction St. Thomas goes on to add:

... when it is said that God *knows* or *knew this future thing*, a cer-

---

[32] Thomas Aquinas, *Summa Theologica*, I, Q. 14, a. 13.
[33] Thomas Aquinas, *Summa Contra Gentiles*, I, Ch. 67, p. 2.
[34] Georg von Wright, *An Essay in Modal Logic* (Amsterdam, North Holland Publishing Company, 1951), p. 25.
[35] *Ibid.*, p. 33.

tain intermediate point between the divine knowledge and the thing known is assumed. This is the time when the above words are spoken, in relation to which time that which is known by God is said to be future. But this is not future with reference to the divine knowledge, which, abiding in the moment of eternity, is related to all things as present to them.[36]

Thus concerning both the idea of God's eternal knowledge of the future and his necessary knowledge of contingents, St. Thomas maintains, as Peirce, that there is a contradiction here only if "we conceive God's knowledge to be among the things which exist at a present time".[37] But since all things are present to God in one eternal vision, then his knowledge is not at *a* present time, but eternal. As such he knows the future in all its actuality since all time is eternally present to him and even though aspects of the temporal series be contingent, he knows the series necessarily and with certainty since he knows it as eternally present.

On these two issues, I think St. Thomas is quite right; the traditional conception of the omniscience of God does not necessarily run into serious difficulty simply at the point of God's knowledge of the future nor at the point of modality. Rather the major difficulty lies elsewhere – in the nature of temporal succession itself and God's manner of knowing upon which St. Thomas's solution rests. Let me clarify what I take to be the major difficulty in the classical position by examining four statements from St. Thomas. They are:

I.   Whoever knows a thing perfectly must know all that can occur to it.[38]

II. The duration of time is stretched out through the succession of before and after.[39]

III. He is ... an ever-abiding simultaneous whole – which belongs to the nature of eternity.[40]

[36]   Thomas Aquinas, *Summa Contra Gentiles*, I, Ch. 67, p. 9.
[37]   Peirce, IV, p. 67.
[38]   Thomas Aquinas, *Summa Theologica*, I, Q. 14, a. 10.
[39]   Thomas Aquinas, *Summa Contra Gentiles*, I, Ch. 66, p. 7.
[40]   *Ibid.*, I, Ch. 66, p. 7.

IV. God sees all things in one thing alone, which is Himself.[41]

The first statement concerns perfect knowledge, or more explicitly omniscience. If God did not know all that does or can occur to a thing, then he certainly could not be said to have perfect knowledge. To know the essential characteristics of a man, for example, is not to know an individual unique man. To know an individual man perfectly would certainly mean to know all that does or can occur to him. And if God did not know individuals in this manner, he would certainly not be said to be omniscient. The second statement merely expresses what is meant by time in this discussion. Any entity "in time" would involve duration and supersession, or succession of before and after. Statement three is an expression of the eternality of God, who is "without beginning and end, having His whole being at once".[42] As such, he is interpreted as being changeless and immutable. And since God's understanding is his being and essence, the cause of all things, then "the knowledge of God is to all creatures what the knowledge of the artificer is to things made by his art".[43] Consequently, God knows the creatures, his effects, in himself. This idea finds expression in statement four, which St. Thomas illustrates with two analogies: ". . . if the center knew itself it would know all lines that proceed from the center; or if light knew itself, it would know all colors".[44]

All four of these statements seem to be essential to St. Thomas's position. A problem, however, arises if we take statements one and two in conjunction with statements three and four. If we accept the first two statements, then it would seem to follow that an omniscient being must know temporal occurrences, both with duration and succession of before and after; for, as we saw earlier and as the Doctor admits, supersession is as much a characteristic of a temporal occurrence or entity as is duration.

[41] Thomas Aquinas, *Summa Theologica*, I, Q. 14, a. 7.
[42] Thomas Aquinas, *Summa Contra Gentiles*, I, Ch. 15, p. 2.
[43] Thomas Aquinas, *Summa Theologica*, I, Q. 14, a. 8.
[44] *Ibid.*, I, Q. 14, 6.

Thus it seems to follow that if time is not an illusion, then perfect knowledge, or omniscience, must include knowledge of supersession. On the other hand, if we take statements three and four together, it seems to follow that God must know all occurrences, not as superseding one another, but as a contemporaneous whole. St. Thomas himself, for example, concludes: "Therefore God sees all things together, not successively." [45] And even more emphatically, he states: "Although contingent things become actual successively, nevertheless God knows contingent things not successively, as they are in their own being, as we do, but simultaneously." [46] If we conceive of perfect knowledge as involving knowledge of supersession, then it follows that the God conceived in statements three and four is not omniscient. If, however, we insist that the God of the last two statements is omniscient and has *perfect* knowledge, then we are forced to admit that supersession, an essential characteristic of the temporal series, and with it duration, is an illusion, for it is not included in perfect knowledge. Thus it seems that the Angelic Doctor's position forces us into a dilemma: Either we confess that God is not omniscient or we must admit that time is unreal. To accept the first horn of the dilemma may have been acceptable to Aristotle, but it would hardly be acceptable to the Christian. For one could raise serious doubts as to whether the conception of a God who does not know individuals perfectly is at all what Christian men, at least, have meant by the word. If, however, we accept the second horn of the dilemma, then it seems that we are forced to agree with a rather curious statement by Bertrand Russell: "The importance of time is rather practical than theoretical, rather in relation to our desires than in relation to truth." [47]

Such a conception of God and time has serious implications, also, for religion. One of the major elements in worship is the act of sacrifice – the contributing to that which inspires our total

---

[45] *Ibid.*, I, Q. 14, a. 7.
[46] *Ibid.*, I, Q. 14, a. 13.
[47] B. Russell, *Mysticism and Logic* (Garden City, N.Y., Doubleday and Company, 1957), p. 20.

commitment and devotion. If we cannot change the content of God's experience and knowledge, how can it be said that we can contribute anything to him. Gilson, for example, writes: "... it it, therefore, some operation in God which will form his beatitude".[48] For we can contribute nothing to his happiness? To contribute, if it means anything, means to add something which was not there before. And is not Hartshorne right when he says of religion, "the basic religious view is that man's good acts and happiness have a value to the supreme being which our bad acts and misery do not".[49] Unless our moral acts and religious acts of worship can contribute something real to the knowledge and experience of God which was not there *before,* in short, unless time is real, morality and religion are in danger of becoming less than empty gestures; they are in danger of becoming a meaningless activity and a sham.

This problem, likewise, has particularly crucial consequences for the Christian religion. At the heart of the Christian religion lies an historical event – the incarnation. If temporal succession is an illusion, then the events forming the drama of the incarnation, crucifixion and resurrection are in danger of becoming no more than a play of shadows, having no reality and no efficacy in history. The mission and destiny of the Christian church, likewise, cannot be taken seriously, for the redemption of the world turns out to be no more than a vain hope concerned with a mere figment of the imagination, a play of our desires, having no relation to truth. If any religion has ever attempted to take time seriously, it has been the Christian religion. Thus it would seem that a conception of God which results in making time unreal, is open to the same question which the first alternative raised: Is such a conception of God at all what Christian men, at least in their acts of worship, have meant by God? The Christian faith not only insists, to use Whitehead's phrase, that *we* take time seriously, it maintains that we should take time seriously because

[48]   Gilson, p. 119.
[49]   Hartshorne, pp. 134-135.

God himself takes time seriously. Is this not a central aspect of the meaning of the incarnation?

There have been many attempts in Christian thought to solve this problem of God and time by retreating to some form of irrationalism. Kierkegaard's embracing of the "absolute paradox" is not only a prime example of this retreat, but one which attempts to turn it into a virtue. It does not help, as some less stout-hearted do, to attempt to make this position more palatable by proposing that a paradox is not really a logical contradiction. The proponents of irrationalism want it to be precisely that. Emil Brunner, for example, writes: "The hall-mark of logical inconsistency clings to all genuine pronouncements of faith." [50]

One may call logical inconsistencies, or contradictions, provocative or interesting, and find some virtue in them, but there is a serious question as to whether or not, by any stretch of the usual meaning of the word 'true', one can call a contradiction true. This much, however, is certain; it is pointless to propose rational arguments against a Tertullian. For at this point rational discussion becomes impossible. To embrace a contradiction, or a logical inconsistency, is to sacrifice the canons of rationality, and to do this is to break off communication. For this reason, I think, one can seriously doubt whether or not this sacrifice of the canons of rationality, even upon the altar of God, is a sacrifice wholly acceptable in his sight.

There is, however, an alternative interpretation of God and omniscience which follows Whitehead's admonition to take time seriously, and an interpretation which itself needs to be taken seriously. This view maintains that the content of God's knowledge changes with the changing, contingent facts of the world. If omniscience means to know, at any moment, all that there is to know and if time is not an illusion, then to know future contingents as indetermined and future, relative to some past and fully determined actuality, is certainly an acceptable meaning of the term 'omniscience'. But does this imply that God is ignorant

[50] Emil Brunner, *Philosophy of Religion from the Standpoint of Protestant Theology* (London, James Clarke and Company, Ltd., 1958), p. 55.

of the future. No; as Hartshorne points out, ". . . this implies that he [is] 'ignorant' *only* if it is assumed that events are there to be known prior to their happenings."[51]

These considerations have led Whitehead to distinguish the two aspects of God which were mentioned earlier. There is what he has called the primordial nature which is eternal, impassible and unchanging. As such it is a necessary condition for the existence of any entity whatsoever and is conditioned by none. The other aspect, which he calls God's consequent nature, is composed of the particular concrete states of God's knowledge and is conditioned by the particular contingent facts in the temporal process. As such, the consequent nature is passible and changes as new facts are added to the divine knowledge. But as the consequent nature changes, nothing is lost, for both past and future are contained in his knowledge, not as an eternal present, or a contemporaneous whole, but to use St. Augustine's terminology, there is the "present of things past, a present of things present, and a present of things future".[52] The present of things past is his memory of past states of the world; the present of things present is his immediate knowledge of the contemporary state of the world; and the present of things future is his expectation of the future contingent states of the world. Although, in a real sense, this view places time *in* God, it does not make God a temporal entity or place God in time. For even though the primordial nature does not dictate exactly what elements shall compose the consequent nature of God, this is done by the contingent events which compose the actual world; it does, however, dictate that there be *some* consequent state of God's knowledge. Thus God is always superseded by himself, and consequently, he has no beginning nor end in time. In this sense, he completely transcends the temporal flux.

[51] Hartshorne, p. 98.
[52] Augustine, *The Confessions*, xi, 20. All quotations from *The Confessions* are taken from the J. G. Pilkington translation in *Basic Writings of Saint Augustine*, edited by Whitney J. Oates (New York, Random House, 1948).

There are at least three serious objections to this view which must be considered. One concerns the religious adequacy of such a conception of omniscience, the second the religious adequacy of a God conditioned by finitude, and the other concerns the attribute of omnipotence. A consideration of these difficulties should help to clarify this alternative conception of the Diety.

The problem of the religious adequacy of this alternative view of omniscience concerns the notion of providence: Does such a view of God's omniscience, which does not include a detailed knowledge of the future, constitute sufficient knowledge for a conception of providence, which seems to be essential for religion. This is a rather difficult question to answer. Yet it would seem that a perfect knowledge of all future possibility and of all past and present actuality would be sufficient for a doctrine of providence. At least it would be difficult to argue that more than this is demanded by religious tradition. But as we have seen, to demand more than this appears to be disastrous.

It might also be argued that such a view places the finite and contingent in God in such a way that he is conditioned to a point that he is inadequate for religion. For is he not like us, bearing the marks of finitude? Tillich, for example, writes concerning the idea of creatures conditioning God,

My resistence against this doctrine ... is rooted in the overwhelming impression of the divine majesty as witnessed by classical religion. This makes any structural dependence of God on something contingent impossible for me to accept.[53]

But this, I think, is to misunderstand the way in which creaturely contingency conditions God. The question is not that of the structural dependence of God. God *qua* God, that is, God in his primordial nature and existence, is not conditioned by anything. He cannot be superseded or become anything other than God and, as such, he is a necessary condition for the structure and existence of anything else. It is only the concrete states of his

[53]   *The Theology of Paul Tillich*, edited by C. W. Kegley and R. W. Bretall (New York, Macmillan and Company, 1956), p. 340.

8

118   AN EXPLICATION OF THE TERM 'GOD'

knowledge that are conditioned by his creatures. This distinction between the conditioned and unconditioned in God and its religious implications has been expressed with great sensitivity by Hartshorne in *Man's Vision of God*:

Self-preservation is not a problem for the necessary being. God "needs" only one thing from the creatures; the intrinsic beauty of their lives, that is, their own true happiness, which is also his happiness through his perfect appreciation of theirs. . . . God "needs" happiness in which to share, not because the alternative is for him to cease to be, for this is not a possible alternative, but because the exact beauty of his own life varies with the amount of beauty in lives generally.[54]

Such a view does not seem in any way to diminish "the overwhelming impression of the divine majesty as witnessed by classical religion"; on the contrary, it seems to give it adequate expression.

D. OMNIPOTENCE AND THE OTHER ATTRIBUTES

The third difficulty, that concerning God's attribute of omnipotence, may be put in this way: If there really are contingent and free creatures that can influence God, then how can it be said that God is all-powerful, or that he has all power? And can anything less than an all-powerful being deserve the name God? It must be honestly admitted that God cannot be said to have all power or to be all-powerful if he is in a real sense dependent upon the power of the creatures and their free choices as this alternative view of God suggests. Before, however, we too hastily condemn this view on this point, let us take as words of caution two statements, one from Whitehead and the other from St. Thomas. In *Modes of Thought*, Whitehead warns us: "The glorification of power has broken more hearts than it has healed." [55] The traditional, and well-intentioned, eagerness to pay God a meta-

---

[54] Hartshorne, p. 163.
[55] A. N. Whitehead, *Modes of Thought* (New York, G. P. Putnam's Sons, 1958), p. 55.

physical compliment by ascribing to him all power is perhaps something which needs some restraint. The sheer glorification of power and the attributing of all power to God, as Whitehead suggests, is perhaps not as complimentary as some would have us think. For if we attribute to God all power, then we become face to face with the ever-recurring question of evil: How can we reconcile the fact that God has all power with the fact of evil and suffering in his creation and, at the same time, preserve his goodness? Although this is not the place to attempt to offer a solution to the problem of evil, it is safe to say that the possibilities of an acceptable solution to the problem are remote indeed, if one insists upon holding to the doctrine that God has all power.

The second statement comes from the *Summa Theologica*: "All confess that God is omnipotent; but it seems difficult to explain in what his omnipotence precisely consists. For there may be a doubt as to the precise meaning of the word 'all' when we say God can do all things." [56] St. Thomas is quite right; the general use of the word 'omnipotent' is quite ambiguous, and some meanings ascribed to it are indeed self-contradictory. Hartshorne has suggested that the very idea that God has "all power over us" is itself self-contradictory. If God has *all* power, then the power of the creatures is totally swallowed up in the power of the supreme being, and there is literally nothing for him to have power over: ". . . 'power over us' would not be power over *us*", he writes, "if our natures and actions counted for nothing." [57] This is not a mere bit of sophistry. To count for nothing, to make no difference, is literally to be nothing. And to make a difference can mean no less than to make a difference to God. Thus the very idea of God's having all power over his creatures is self-contradictory, for if he had all power, there could be no creatures to have power over.

As St. Thomas has suggested, one obvious limitation on the 'all' in omnipotence is logical impossibility: ". . . whatever implies contradiction does not come within the scope of divine omnipo-

---

[56]   Thomas Aquinas, *Summa Theologica*, I, Q. 25, p. 3.
[57]   Hartshorne, p. 294.

tence, because it cannot have the aspect of possibility".[58] All that omnipotence could consistently mean would be all logically possible power. And if omnipotence is interpreted in this way, then there is no conflict between this alternative conception of the Diety and the attribute of omnipotence. If there are real free and contingent creatures, it would be logically impossible for God to make their decisions for them, for they would not then be the choices of the creatures. The limitations imposed upon God's power by the choices of the creatures are no more than the limitations of logical impossibility.

In order to clarify this conception of God's omnipotence, we need to make a distinction between the power to exist and the power to be in a particular concrete state of existence. The bare fact that I exist, for example, is one thing; the fact that I exist here and now with these particular thoughts and these particular feelings is something quite different. The first is obviously a necessary condition for the second, but not vice versa. I can have different thoughts and different feelings at some other place and some other time and still exist. According to this alternative conception of the power of God, God is dependent upon nothing for his power to exist; he exists necessarily. He is, however, dependent upon the free choices of his creatures for the particular character of the concrete state of his knowledge at any one moment. Thus omnipotence means that the existence of God cannot be threatened by any power whatsoever, and since God is a necessary condition for the existence of anything else, his power extends to every creature. As Gilson expressed it, "let the divine act-of-being cease for a moment to keep things existing, and there is nothing".[59] The only limitations imposed upon God's power are the limitations of logical impossibility, one of which is that God cannot make the free decisions of the creatures. But since God exists necessarily, no matter what the free choices of the creatures might be, they can never imperil the existence of God, nor ultimately frustrate his purposes.

[58]   Thomas Aquinas, *Summa Theologica*, I, Q. 25, 3.
[59]   Gilson, p. 101.

The positive value of this alternative to the classical conception of diety is the fact that it takes time seriously; rather, it holds that God himself takes time seriously. Both past and future are in God. The past is there as actualized and settled fact, but the future is indeterminate even to God. Consequently, we are called upon to take the future seriously. It is partly the responsibility of human beings with their free decisions and actions to settle this indeterminateness which characterizes the future. In so doing we contribute not only to its outcome, but we contribute something of value or disvalue to God. "Freedom is", as Hartshorne writes, "our opportunity and our tragic destiny." [60] In so far as our choices and actions are a response to God's creative purposes, he rejoices with us. In so far as our choices and actions fall short and conflict with the choices and actions of other creatures, there is suffering and evil; but God is far from impassible, he becomes, in Whitehead's words, "the fellow sufferer who understands".[61] And herein lies our hope: No matter how far short we may fall, we can never frustrate his purposes, and despite the inescapable perpetual perishing which characterizes the temporal flux, nothing cherished is ever lost, for every accomplishment of value is contained forever in him as actualized fact.

The problem of omnipresence is simple. If we take omnipresence to mean "present in all", then only that being who is the necessary condition for every creature can truly be said to be omnipresent. His goodness, knowledge, and power extend to every creature. Where he is not, there is nothing.

It remains to be seen what can be said concerning the traditional properties of infinity, simplicity, and immutability in relation to God as he has been explicated. It is obvious that if these terms are taken, as they frequently are, as simple negations of finitude, complexity, and change, then none of them can be predicated of God according to our definite description. For example, in the discussion of omniscience, it was maintained that God included finitude, complexity, and change. If, however, we

[60]   Charles Hartshorne, *Logic of Perfection*, p. 14.
[61]   Whitehead, *Process and Reality*, p. 532.

take these notions as polar opposites, then all of them can be predicated of God. His abstract nature can be said to be infinite, simple, and immutable; while finitude, complexity, and change can be predicated of his concrete nature.

It should be noted that all of the properties and attributes which have been discussed concern what we have called God's general nature – that is, they express his relations to any and every creature, or event. Take omniscience, for example; it does not matter what a particular event might be, God knows it. Consequently our explicatum, statements concerning the existence of this supreme being, and statements concerning God's attributes would all be statements of natural theology, and, consequently, metaphysics. It is the task of the natural theologian to see if these cannot be formulated in a formal metaphysical language. If this can be done, then natural theology has met the challenge of the 'philosophical revolution". This is not an easy task. Nevertheless, it seems to be the proper and most effective way of approaching the problem of natural theology; and, if theology is to meet the challenge of contemporary philosophy, it seems to be the *only* way. As an illustration of what might be done with this approach, let us examine more specifically the problem of a formal language for metaphysics.

VI

LANGUAGE AND THE TASK OF METAPHYSICS

The term, 'metaphysics', has had a rather unhappy history. It had a less than romantic or exalted beginning, signifying no more than a position in a list: "after the Physics". But from that lowly beginning the term became the accepted title of that science which dealt with the first principles of all the sciences and with being *qua* being. Today, however, it has come to be in many places a term of disrespect, signifying any form of otherworldliness, wild speculation or sheer nonsense. If the term itself has had an unhappy history, so has that queen of the sciences which it was used to christen. In the *Critique of Pure Reason,* Kant speaks of the Queen in this way: "... the changed fashion of the time brings her only scorn; a matron outcast and forsaken, she mourns like Hecuba".[1] If she mourned in Kant's day, how she must wail today.

In response to a suggestion by Gottfried Martin[2] that we distinguish between the search for first principles, *scientia universalis,* and a theory of being, *ontologia generalis,* assigning the problem of first principles to logic and allow metaphysics to concentrate on ontology, Richard Martin argues that the two "seem so indissolubly intertwined as to justify the maxim: No ontology, no logic".[3] If logic is conceived of as anything other than an uninterpreted calculus, then Richard Martin is certainly right. In Chapter III we suggested that the metaphysical task

---

[1] Kant, *Critique of Pure Reason,* pp. 7-8.
[2] Gottfried Martin, "Metaphysics as *Scientia Universalis* and as *Ontologia Generalis*", *The Relevance of Whitehead,* editor, Ivor Leclerc (London, Allen and Unwin, 1961), pp. 219-231.
[3] Richard Martin, "Ontology, Category-Words, and Modal Logic", *Process and Divinity,* editors W. L. Reese and Eugene Freeman (Lasalle, Open Court, 1964), p. 272.

was that of constructing a linguistic framework for describing the common world disclosed in experience. Such a framework would be logic in its most general and comprehensive application to that which is and the provable, or necessary, statements in such a framework could justifiably be called first principles. In speaking of modern logic and metaphysics, Richard Martin goes on to say: "Each is here to stay. Not peaceful co-existence but intimate collaboration should be aimed at, for which the time seems ripe." [4] If Richard Martin is right, and I think he is, then the time is perhaps ripe for reopening Kant's question: How is metaphysics possible? It is far too much to hope for an immediate restoration of the Queen of the sciences to her proper place, perhaps the most that we can hope for as yet is to indicate a possible way back to her throne.

A.   THE METAPHYSICAL TASK

For the purposes of explicating the metaphysical task let us look at a definition given by a twentieth century metaphysician. In the opening chapter of *Process and Reality,* Whitehead writes, "Speculative Philosophy is the endeavour to frame a coherent, logical, necessary system of general ideas in terms of which every element of our experience can be interpreted." [5] Ignoring for the present any distinction which Whitehead may make between metaphysics and speculative philosophy, let us examine this definition.

By 'interpreted' Whitehead means that "everything of which we are conscious, as enjoyed, perceived, willed, or thought, shall have the character of a particular instance of the general scheme".[6] Interpretation, however, is the task of both science and philosophy as he sees them. In *Adventures of Ideas* he writes: "They are both concerned with the understanding of individual facts as

---

[4]   *Ibid.,* p. 273.
[5]   A. N. Whitehead, *Process and Reality,* p. 4.
[6]   *Ibid.,* p. 4.

illustrations of general principles. The principles are understood in the abstract, and the facts are understood in respect to their embodiment of the principle." [7] The difference between the two lies in the universality of the principles of metaphysics. For this reason Whitehead adds to the two internal criteria of 'logical' and 'coherent' the two external criteria for metaphysical interpretation: 'applicable' and 'adequate'. It is the latter which assures the universality of the scheme. Rather than attempt any historical or systematic justification of this definition, I shall merely develop the definition and leave it to the reader to judge its historical adequacy.

By 'coherence' Whitehead means that "the fundamental ideas, in terms of which the scheme is developed, presuppose each other so that in isolation they are meaningless".[8] To call them 'meaningless' in isolation does not mean that it is necessary for these notions to be defined in terms of each other, but it does mean that "what is indefinable in one such notion cannot be abstracted from its relevance to the other notions".[9] This criterion is no more than an expression of the harmony of rational thought and an interpretation of the essential relatedness of things in experience; that is, the "fundamental notions shall not seem capable of abstraction from each other" and "no entity can be conceived in complete abstraction from the system of the universe".[10]

Perhaps the best way to understand what Whitehead means by 'coherence' is to consider his discussion of 'incoherence', which he defines as "the arbitrary disconnection of first principles".[11] The key word here is 'arbitrary'. 'Arbitrary disconnection' implies, as Leclerc points out, "that there is no principle more general in terms of which they can be brought together – the

[7] A. N. Whitehead, *Adventures of Ideas* (New York, Macmillan, 1933), p. 144.
[8] Whitehead, *Process and Reality*, p. 5.
[9] *Ibid.*, p. 5.
[10] *Ibid.*, p. 5.
[11] *Ibid.*, p. 9.

word 'arbitrary' stresses that there is no 'reason' for the disconnection".[12] In this sense incoherence is the collapse of the rationalistic endeavor, which is an expression of "the faith that at the
base of things we shall not find mere arbitrary mystery".[13]

The rational coherence of the system naturally implies that it
be 'logical'. And Whitehead tells us that by 'logical' he means
no more than is ordinarily meant: "logical consistency, or lack
of contradiction, the definitions of constructs in logical terms,
the exemplification of general logical notions in specific instances,
and the principles of inference".[14] This is an expression of the
faith that "the harmony of logic lies upon the universe as an iron
necessity".[15] The only alternative is irrationalism.

The two criteria governing 'interpretation' are defined in this
way: " 'applicable' means that some items of experience are thus
interpretable, and 'adequate' means that there are no items in-
capable of such interpretation".[16] The first criterion preserves
the empirical emphasis; it insists that the system has its origin
in generalizations based on the analytic observations of components in experience. The second criterion, on the other hand,
insists that the applicability of the notions be spread beyond the
restricted locus in which they originated. A primary notion derived, for example, from physics finds its justification as a metaphysical notion when it finds successful application in fields
beyond physics. This is no more than the insistence upon the
complete generality of metaphysical notions contained in the
phrase, "in terms of which every element of our experience can
be interpreted".

It is this complete generality of the metaphysical ideas which
gives meaning to the term 'necessary'. They are necessarily embodied in all things, or as Whitehead puts it in *Religion in the*

[12]   Ivor Leclerc, *Whitehead's Metaphysics* (New York, Macmillan, 1958),
p. 35.
[13]   A. N. Whitehead, *Science and the Modern World* (New York, The
New American Library, 1948), p. 27.
[14]   Whitehead, *Process and Reality*, p. 5.
[15]   Whitehead, *Science and the Modern World*, p. 28.
[16]   Whitehead, *Process and Reality*, p. 4.

Making, they "are indispensably relevant to everything that happens".[17] This gives meaning to the assertion that metaphysical principles are not contingent. Contingency is the mark of principles which have a restricted applicability. In contrast to necessary principles, they may or may not be embodied, or relevant.

Conceived in this way, metaphysics is both rational and empirical. It is rational in that it is an expression of an ultimate faith in reason; that is, "the truth that the ultimate nature of things lie together in a harmony which excludes mere arbitrariness".[18] This rationalism, however, is balanced by an equally strong empiricism, for it assumes that the elucidation of immediate experience is the sole justification of any thought and that immediate experience is its only starting point. Metaphysics, so conceived, does not start from clear, distinct, and certain principles. This is what Whitehead means when he writes that "philosophy is the search for premises. It is not deduction." [19] Even the rationalistic faith is not a self-evident metaphysical premise; "it is the faith which forms the motive for the pursuit of all sciences alike, including metaphysics".[20] And even it must spring "from direct inspection of the nature of things as disclosed in our own immediate present experience".[21] Consequently, the verification of a rationalistic system can only be found in its general success in interpreting experience, "not in the peculiar certainty, or initial clarity, of its first principles".[22]

B.   METAPHYSICS AS A FORMAL LANGUAGE

Given this view of metaphysics, the question of its language naturally arises. Its abstract nature and its role of interpretation,

---

[17] A. N. Whitehead, *Religion in the Making* (New York, Macmillan, 1926), p. 72, footnote.
[18] Whitehead, *Science and the Modern World*, p. 27.
[19] A. N. Whitehead, *Modes of Thought* (New York, Macmillan, 1926), p. 143.
[20] Whitehead, *Process and Reality*, p. 67.
[21] Whitehead, *Science and the Modern World*, p. 27.
[22] Whitehead, *Process and Reality*, p. 12.

as we defined it, immediately suggests the possibility of constructing a formal symbolic language for metaphysics – that is, a formal system of signs and rules for their use by means of which the general ideas and their relations can be formulated and tested for their consistency. By interpretation we meant that certain individual facts are taken to be particular instances or embodiments of general abstract principles: "The principles are understood in the abstract, and the facts are understood in respect to their embodiment of the principles." [23] This is precisely the role of a formal language. In a formal symbolic language abstract conditions are set up such that if they hold in any case of a certain type, we conclude that they hold in a certain particular case of this type. To argue for a formal language for metaphysics is no more than to argue that metaphysics is an ideal abstract language and an interpreted formal schema is the most efficient abstract language that we have. With Bergmann we can conceive of the metaphysical problem as the task of constructing an "ideal language" which can "account for all areas of our experience".[24]

In suggesting the application of formal symbolic systems to metaphysics, it must be pointed out that this in no way makes metaphysics a deductive science. It is constructive, rather than deductive. The metaphysician, as we have suggested, would not begin with self-evident postulates and, in his formal language, deduce metaphysical propositions. Alternate metaphysical languages with different primitive terms and postulates are no doubt possible. It is the metaphysicians' task to investigate the possibilities, to construct languages, and to judge them by the four metaphysical criteria. The deductive element in a formal language, in so far as metaphysics is concerned, is trivial. It only assures us that the language is 'logical'; and 'logicality' is only one of the four criteria.

Since this approach to metaphysics, conceiving it as a formal language, may appear to be something of a radical approach,

---

[23] Whitehead, *Adventures of Ideas*, p. 144.
[24] Gustav Bergmann, *The Metaphysics of Logical Positivism*, p. 40.

perhaps something should be said concerning its relation to natural language. All metaphysical systems, so far as I know, have been constructed in natural languages. There is, also, a large group of contemporary philosophers who seem to think that philosophical analysis should concern itself only with the analysis of the common usages of words and statements in a natural language. How can we justify what seems to be a radical approach? First, to advocate the formalization of a metaphysical language is in no way to deny the usefulness of the analysis of natural language. A philosophical study of natural languages and the common usages of words is no doubt a valuable investigation, but as Quine points out, "it passes over, as irrelevant, one important aspect of philosophical analysis – the creative aspect, which is involved in the progressive refinement of scientific language".[25] It is the idea of "progressive refinement" which lures us to investigate the possibility of constructing a formal metaphysical language. Ordinary language will, however, always remain in the background and fundamental. Construction does not preclude analysis, for, as Richard Martin points out, "logical complexities and logical systems are not dreamed up artifically; they are simply there, embedded in natural language, as it were, waiting to be brought to light and suitably characterized".[26] The only argument for formalization is efficiency.

The general advantages of constructing a formalized symbolic language have been successfully argued by Martin in his book, *Truth and Denotation*.[27] These include 'clarity and precision', 'an aid to intuition', 'a corrective to faulty thinking', 'a full specification of assumptions', 'logical efficiency', etc. The arguments are well known and well established, and they need not be repeated here. Our primary concern is to determine the peculiar advantages of formalization in metaphysics as we have defined it. The most

[25]   W. V. Quine, *From a Logical Point of View* (Cambridge, Harvard University Press, 1953), p. 106.

[26]   Richard Martin, *Intension and Decision* (Englewood Cliffs, N.J., Prentice-Hall, Inc., 1963), p. 153.

[27]   Richard Martin, *Truth and Denotation* (Chicago, University of Chicago Press, 1958), pp. 8-15.

effective way of seeing these advantages is to examine the possibility of constructing a formal metaphysical language in relation
to the four criteria given by Whitehead for a metaphysical system.

A formal language has two elements which we will call a
logical calculus, a formal syntactical schema, and an extralogical
base, its interpretation. The criterion of logicality concerns what I
have called the logical calculus of the language. This criterion certainly points to the advantage of a formalized language. Of course,
anything which can be formulated in a formal language can likewise
be stated in an ordinary natural language. A language, however,
with a logical syntax, such as a metaphysical language, has certain definite advantages when formalized. In contrast to ordinary
language, in a formal language, the signs are somewhat less
ambiguous and the formulations are more exact; therefore, the
purity and correctness of a derivation can be tested with greater
ease and accuracy. Despite the fact that logical errors, as such,
in metaphysics are perhaps trivial in so far as the history of
metaphysics is concerned, it cannot be doubted that in so far as
our criterion of logicality is important, formalization is a distinct
advantage.

Formalization, however, is an even more useful tool, as we
shall see, when we consider the criterion of coherence. Just as
the criterion of logicality concerns primarily the logical calculus
of the ideal, or metaphysical language, I would suggest that the
criterion of coherence is concerned with the extralogical basis
of the language, that is, its descriptive predicates and their
axioms. Here the problem might be divided into systematic and
extra-systematic coherence. To define a predicate of a language
in terms of more primitive predicates, as is done in a formal
language, is to interrelate the predicates as well as to simplify the
basis for the language. Thus, to seek economy in a language is
not done merely for the sake of superficial neatness, for every
definition formulated in a system increases the coherence within the
system. To quote Goodman, "To economize and to systematize
are the same thing." [28]

[28]   Nelson Goodman, *Structure of Appearance*, p. 59.

This, however, not only assures us of coherence within the system, it makes clear the particular problem of extra-systematic coherence, or coherence among the primitives of the language. For example, suppose we, as Bergmann seems to suggest,[29] take both mental and physical predicates as primitives. Unless we can give some extra-systematic way of relating, or justifying, two un-related primitives, we can be accused of Cartesian dualism, and consequently, of violating the coherence criterion. It would be a clear case of "arbitrary disconnection". Since only by formaliza-tion can we be sure of all the abstract conditions which we have presupposed, it would seem that only by formalization can we both be assured of coherence within the language and make precise the problem of extra-systematic coherence. For only by formalizing a language can we be certain of all primitives and their axioms.

It is, however, when we come to the criteria of applicability and adequacy that the advantages of formalization become most exciting. It is these criteria, particularly the criterion of adequacy, which seem most difficult when it comes to evaluating a meta-physical system. The criterion of applicability can easily be ex-plicated in terms of semantical interpretation. Does the system have an interprtation in experience? If so, the criterion of ap-plicability is satisfied. But the problem of determining if "every-thing of which we are conscious, as enjoyed, perceived, willed, or thought", has "the character of a particular instance of the general scheme" seems a hopeless task. But formalization has the possibilities of offering us a very effective tool for applying these two criteria.

In the "Preface" to *Process and Reality* Whitehead writes "that it must be one of the motives of a complete cosmology to construct a system of ideas which bring the aesthetic, moral, and religious interests into relation with those concepts of the world which have their origin in natural science".[30] And, as we have suggested, it is the metaphysician's task to construct this system

[29]   Bergmann, pp. 132-152.
[30]   Whitehead, *Process and Reality*, p. vi.

of ideas. If a metaphysical language could be formulated which would form the basis for a language of the natural sciences and, at the same time, be a language in which aesthetic, ethical, and religious statements could be formulated, would this not come very near to offering an interpretation of "everything of which we are conscious, an enjoyed, perceived, willed or thought?" For certainly the observations of the enjoyments, perceptions, willings, and thoughts of man are found in his natural science, his morals, his aesthetics, and his religion.

In the first place, we already have an abstract language which has become almost universal in its applications in the natural sciences – mathematics. The importance and fruitfulness of the application of mathematics here is indubitable. Thus, one criterion of adequacy must be that the ideal, or metaphysical, language be strong enough to include classical mathematics. This gives us a very definite criterion for choosing the extralogical calculus for the language. The other problem is that of constructing definitions, or predicates, that will be universally applicable in these four areas of science, aesthetics, ethics, and religion. If sufficient work could be done in the applications of formal languages in these areas, this would help to determine the primitive predicates necessary for each of these areas. The metaphysical problem, then, would be to find even more general primitive predicates in terms of which these specialized primitives could be defined. In this way we would have a precise way of checking the adequacy of the general metaphysical ideas – to see if they really are adequate for interpreting every area of experience.

Perhaps the best justification that can be given for conceiving the metaphysical task in terms of constructing a linguistic framework for describing the common world disclosed to us in experience, comes precisely in the nature of the problems which arise when one attempts this type of construction.[31] Gustov Berg-

---

[31] For a relevant discussion of a possible relation of the traditional problem of metaphysical categories and contemporary linguistic frameworks see Richard Martin, "Ontology, Category-Words, and Modal Logic". *Process and Divinity*, pp. 273-280.

mann[32] has pointed out that the decisions which one must face in constructing an ideal language reflect many of the traditional metaphysical positions. Although I disagree, as I shall point out later, with many of Bergmann's conclusions, I think his basic thesis is sound. And this will, I think, become evident when we discuss the various decisions which must be made when one attempts to set up such a linguistic framework.

C. THE CHOICE OF A LOGICAL CALCULUS AND MATHEMATICAL BASE

The first step in constructing a formal language for metaphysics is the choice of the logical calculus, or what Goodman calls "the general apparatus of the system".[33] Of necessity this would include a basic logic, for example, a sentential (or propositional) calculus and a lower functional calculus. In addition, such a language would probably need to include either a calculus of classes or some axioms for a theory of sets.

It has frequently been taken for granted that the logical calculus of a system is purely neutral machinery which carries with it no ontological or philosophical implications. Such a neutrality, however, can be preserved only if the logical calculus is left uninterpreted. For, as Goodman, Quine,[34] and others have argued, if one uses variables which are construed as having entities of any given kind as values, he commits himself to the existence of such entities. Pure quantification theory, of course, need not itself be construed as making any ontological commitments. Its theorems may be viewed not as statements but as schema, or

---

[32]   Bergmann, passim.

[33]   Nelson Goodman, *Structure of Appearance*, p. 30.

[34]   See W. V. Quine, "On Universals", *Journal of Symbolic Logic*, XII (1947), pp. 74-84; W. V. Quine, "Notes on Existence and Necessity", *Journal of Philosophy*, XL (1943), pp. 113-127; W. V. Quine, "Designation and Existence", *Journal of Philosophy*, XXXVI (1939), pp. 701-709; W. V. Quine, *From a Logical Point of View*, passim; and Goodman, *The Structure of Appearance*, pp. 30-41.

diagrams, depicting patterns of true statements. The letters may, in this case, be viewed not as variables but as schematic letters, just as the 'p' and 'q' of truth-function theory may be viewed as schematic letters rather than as variables taking propositions or truth-values as values. When, however, these formulae are considered as statements and the letters in the quantifiers as bound variables – which they must be if we are to have a language – one is committed to the existence of those entities to which the variables of the language must be capable of referring in order that the affirmations made in the theory be true.[35] If one quantifies, for example, over variables which take classes as their values, then he is committed to the existence of classes. To use Quine's cryptic phrase, "To be is to be the value of a variable." [36]

This is not to be taken as asserting that existence is in any way dependent upon language. What is, is. We do not examine a certain language in order to discover what there is, but only in order to determine what the language *asserts* that there is. Quine's thesis only maintains that one cannot deny, for example, the existence of classes and, at the same time, use a language which commits him to the existence of classes. If one's language forces him to admit the existence of classes, he must either accept their existence or change his language.

This problem of the ontological commitment of formal languages has been brought to the fore in contemporary philosophy by the discussions on the foundations of mathematics. These discussions are particularly relevant to the choice of a calculus for the metaphysical language for two reasons:

(1) The work done in the foundations of mathematics gives us a clue to the ontological commitments of various languages.

---

[35] Here we are discussing only those languages which would or would not admit classes as values of variables. This discussion does not consider such alternative logics as combinatory logics. As Quine suggests, however, equivalent criteria might be devised to suit these alternative forms in terms of translatability. See "On Universals", *Journal of Symbolic Logic*, XII (1947), p. 75.
[36] W. V. Quine, "Designation and Existence", *Journal of Philosophy*, XXXVI (1939), p. 708.

The development of alternate foundations has led Quine, and rightly I think, to see certain parallels between the modern schools of logicism, intuitionalism, and formalism among mathematicians and the classical positions of realism, or platonism as he prefers to call it, conceptualism, and nominalism: "Thus it is that the great medieval controversy over universals has flared up anew in the modern philosophy of mathematics." [37] The problem around which the debate centers is the problem of the existence of classes, or abstract entities.

(2) The second point at which these discussions on the foundations of mathematics become relevant for the problem of constructing an ideal language is the criterion of adequacy. If our metaphysical language is to be one in which we can talk about every area of experience, one of the most important things which it must include will be mathematics. Thus, our language must be able to furnish an adequate basis for classical mathematics.

If we take the classical realist's, or platonist's, position on universals to be that our ability to understand general words and to recognize resemblances between concrete objects is inexplicable unless we posit the existence of universals, independent of the mind, as objects of apprehension, then there is a very close parallel between logicism and realism. Logicism condones the use of bound variables to refer indiscriminately to abstract entities, or classes, whether known or unknown, specifiable or unspecifiable. Thus, it commits itself to the existence of these entities, and this existence is quite independent of their being known or specifiable.

Attempts to use a language which quantifies over classes but interprets them so that they do not refer to abstract entities have been, on the whole, unsuccessful. Lazerowitz, for example, writes: ". . . to say that a general word stands for an abstract entity does not mean that it denotes anything other than the concrete particular things to which it is applicable".[38] Such an interpretation

---

[37]   W. V. Quine, *From a Logical Point of View*, p. 13.
[38]   Morris Lazerowitz, "The Existence of Universals", *Mind*, n. s., XL (1946), p. 19.

is a confusion of concrete aggregates, or collections, with classes. As Quine has pointed out, a class of stones and a heap of stones are not the same thing. An aggregate of stones in a heap and the aggregate of molecules in the heap are the same concrete aggregate, but the class of stones in the heap and the class of molecules in the heap are not the same class – they have different members. He concludes: "Classes, therefore, are abstract entities; we may call them aggregates, or collections, if we like, but they are universals." [39] Likewise, Russell's attempt to eliminate the existence of abstract entities by using propositional functions as values of bound variables is equally unsuccessful. In the first place, there is an ambiguity in Russell's use of the phrase, 'propositional function'; sometimes it seems to refer to an open sentence and sometimes to an attribute. It is, however, in the second sense that it is used as values for variables. But attributes are also abstract entities. Consequently, Quine is right; "nothing can be claimed for the theory beyond a reduction of certain universals to others." [40]

Perhaps at this point an alternative view, proposed by Bergmann, concerning the ontological commitment of a language should be mentioned. Bergmann accepts the calculus of classes as a part of the ideal language – in fact, he accepts the logic of the "non-controversial parts" of *Principia Mathematica,* supplemented with adequate descriptive predicates, as the ideal language. But he denies that "the 'There is (exists)' in the quantifier has much to do with the 'existence' which traditional ontology tries to assert".[41] Rather, according to him,[42] the ontological commitment of a language depends upon its undefined descriptive predicates. The traditional nominalist's rejection of universals, for example, has nothing to do with the rejection of classes, rather it is the assertion that the ideal language contains no undefined descriptive signs except proper names.

[39]   W. V. Quine, "On Universals", *Journal of Symbolic Logic,* XII (1947), p. 79.
[40]   *Ibid.,* p. 79.
[41]   Bergmann, p. 242.
[42]   *Ibid.,* p. 40.

Bergmann's purpose in doing this is obvious. Not only does he wish to show that most philosophical disputes are not real disputes, but by limiting the problem of "existence in the onto- logical sense" to the undefined descriptive predicates of the ideal language, he hopes to slavage what he calls the core of traditional nominalism in a language which quantifies over class variables. He limits the undefined descriptive terms to predicates of the first type only, but includes quantification over variables of higher types in order to include classical mathematics. This, he proposes, is a way of explicating what "non-positivistic philosophers may try to express when they insist that while, for example, colors exist, numbers and grammatical categories merely subsist".[43] In other words, the undefined descriptive predicates refer to things that "exist" while the class variables refer to things which "sub- sist".

That Bergmann's view is a more adequate analysis of the traditional ontological meaning of 'exist' is dubious. It seems that predicates as such, either defined or undefined, have little to do with the ontological issue. The problem is: What do the state- ments of the language assert to exist? This is the problem of bound variables. Also, his distinction between "subsistence" and "existence" only confuses the issue between nominalism and realism. What Bergmann is doing is merely making a distinction between abstract and concrete entities, a distinction which no one would deny. This distinction, however, can be made within the ideal language itself: A concrete entity may be defined as an entity which has no members – that is, it is not a class. While an abstract entity may be defined as an entity which has members – a class. There seems to be no intelligible alternative; if one chooses, as the ideal language, a language which allows quantifi- cation over class variables, he has committed himself to a modern type of platonic realism which asserts the existence of an un- limited realm of abstract entities.

If one takes the classical conceptualist's position to be that

---

[43] *Ibid.*, p. 242.

universals are not discovered but constructed by the human mind, there is a close parallel between it and the position of the intuitionists in mathematical theory. For the intuitionists reject unlimited quantification over class variables and countenance the use of bound variables to refer to abstract entities only when these entities are capable of being constructed individually from entities given in advance. Ultimately all mathematical constructions, for them, rest upon the natural numbers, and these, in turn, rest upon a "basal" intuition, which seems to rely upon Kant's notion of the pure form of time. (One is reminded here of Kronecker's remark: "God made the natural numbers; all the rest is man's handiwork.") This limits the existence of abstract entities to those constructed by the human mind. Consequently, the answer to "the question where mathematical exactness exists", is according to Brouwer, "in the human intellect".[44] Thus a conceptualistic language may be explicated as a language in which the bound variables are limited to only those classes which can be constructed by the human mind from entities already given. Consequently, the conceptualist is committed to only those abstract entities which exist in the human mind.

If we interpret classical nominalism as rejecting altogether the existence of a realm of abstract entities, there is a close parallel between it and the mathematical work of the formalists. The formalists refuse to countenance the existence of abstract entities, either of the unbridled sort of the logicists or the man-made sort of the intuitionists. He prefers to keep mathematics as a play of insignificant concrete notations according to a given set of rules. The utility which these notations may have for the physicist or the technologist need not imply significance in any literal linguistic sense – in other words, they need not refer to anything. It is the rules which furnish agreement among mathematicians and have significance, not the symbols.

The consequences of formalism for an ideal language are obvious. If it is an adequate foundation for mathematics, then

[44] L. E. J. Brouwer, "Intuitionism and Formalism", translator Arnold Dresden, *Bulletin of American Mathematical Society*, XX (1913), p. 83.

classes are not needed in the ideal language in order to accommodate mathematics. This suggests the possibility of a nominalistic ideal language – one free from abstract entities altogether. Yet one who wishes to adhere consistently to a nominalistic metaphysical language is faced with three problems: [45] (1) If he renounces all abstract entities, he must be able to exclude all predicates which are not predicates of concrete individuals or definable in terms of predicates of concrete individuals. In addition to predicates of individuals, he must limit himself to individual variables, quantification with respect to these variables, and truth functions. In this way he will avoid all classes. (2) All statements which cannot be formulated in this limited logical calculus, which would include a large part of classical mathematics, he must declare as meaningless – merely strings of insignificant physical marks. (3) Even the syntax of the language and the rules of semantics must be nominalistic – that is, they must make no use of terms or devices which involve commitment to abstract entities.

Thus from the contemporary discussion on the foundations of mathematics, we have clues to three possible alternatives for a logical calculus of the metaphysical language: (1) a realistic language, which would include an interpreted logical calculus with unlimited quantification over class variables, (2) a conceptualistic language, which would include an interpreted logical calculus with only limited quantification over classes, and (3) a nominalistic language, which would reject an interpreted logical calculus with either unlimited or limited quantification over class variables.

Given these three possibilities, quantification over *all, some, no* class variables, how are we to choose between them in constructing our logical calculus for the ideal language? This is the other point at which mathematics becomes relevant to the metaphysical problem. As we have suggested before, the language which can furnish the best foundation for classical mathematics would be the best candidate for the metaphysical language. Any

[45] See Nelson Goodman and W. V. Quine, "Steps Toward a Constructive Nominalism", *Journal of Symbolic Logic*, XII (1947), pp. 105-122.

hope of getting unanimous agreement among mathematicians and philosophers over the meaning of the "best foundation" is probably a vain hope. The choice, nevertheless, is not strictly arbitrary, because it does make a real difference which alternative we choose. The choice, for example, between a realistic and a conceptualistic basis makes a real difference as to just how much of classical mathematics can be included. The realist can, in his language, accommodate all of Cantor's ascending orders of infinity, while a conceptualist must stop at the lowest order of infinity and, as a consequence, abandon even some of the classical laws of real numbers. Also, a nominalist must either regard classical mathematics as discredited or, at best, consider most of it as meaningless but useful notations.

It would seem that the language which could accommodate all of classical mathematics as meaningful would, unless there are serious objections, be the best candidate for the metaphysical language. Consequently, let us examine the objections which are frequently given for rejecting a realistic foundation for mathematics.

Perhaps the weakest reason for refusing to admit abstract entities is given by Goodman and Quine when they write: "Fundamentally this refusal is based on a philosophical intuition that cannot be justified by appeal to anything more ultimate." [46] A dispute can seldom be solved by one side appealing to an "ultimate intuition" – whatever that may mean. All three groups in this case can, in equal fashion, appeal to an "ultimate intuition". As an objection, therefore, such an appeal is very weak and should not be taken too seriously.

Another reason which is frequently given for rejecting or limiting quantification over class variables is the argument for economy. This is a modern version of Occam's Razor. In the name of economy the nominalist wishes to rid his universe entirely of what Goodman calls "a host of ethereal, platonic, pseudo-entities" [47] and the conceptualist, more modestly, wishes to trim

[46]   *Ibid.*, p. 105.
[47]   Goodman, *The Structure of Appearance*, p. 32.

his universe down to only those abstract entities which he can construct. Precisely what economy is, however, is a tricky question. Just where does economy become crippling and cease to be economical? When the conceptualist has to sacrifice the theory of transfinite numbers, is he justified in asserting, as Quine does, "So far, good riddance?" [48] But even more questionable, is he justified in sacrificing what Quine himself calls "certain more traditional and distinctly more desirable theorems of mathematics" [49] such as the proof that every bounded class of real numbers has a least bound? Likewise, is it economical when the nominalist has to declare a large part of mathematical notation to be meaningless? That this is far from ideal is indicated by Goodman himself, an ardent apologist for nominalism: "The devious device of setting up and managing an additional and meaningless language recommends itself *only* where, as in the case of some parts of mathematics, direct translation is so difficult as to seem hopeless." [50] Wilder is quite right in questioning "such a 'state of health' " which "has been achieved by 'cutting off the leg to heal the toe !' " [51] Perhaps there will never be universal agreement on what constitutes real economy, but the modern discussions concerning the foundations of mathematics have made clear the consequences of choosing one of the three alternatives.

The third, and perhaps most important, reason for rejecting realism is the charge that unlimited quantification over class variables leads to paradoxes. That escapes from these paradoxes have been proposed is well known, but it is the escapes themselves which are frequently considered questionable. Goodman and Quine, for example, write: "Escape from these paradoxes can apparently be effected only by recourse to alternative rules whose artificially and arbitrariness arouse suspicion that we are

[48]   Quine, *From a Logical Point of View*, p. 127.
[49]   *Ibid.*, p. 127.
[50]   Goodman, *The Structure of Appearance*, p. 32. (Italics mine.)
[51]   Raymond Wilder, *Introduction to the Foundations of Mathematics* (New York, John Wiley and Sons, 1952), p. 249.

lost in a world of make believe." [52] It is primarily the theory of types whose artificially and arbitrariness arouses suspicion here. On the other hand, as Martin has pointed out, "some logicians think that the distinction of type has a certain 'naturalness' about it and corresponds more or less roughly with intuition".[53] Whether "artificial and arbitrary" or "natural and intuitive", one must agree with Martin when he writes: ". . . type theory has come to be regarded as one of the most important, presumably consistent, methods of providing a logical foundation for mathematics and natural science." [54]

Concerning the nominalists, Carnap writes: "Let us therefore admit that the nominalistic critics may possibly be right. But if so, they will have to offer better arguments than they have so far." [55] The same may be said for the conceptualist. Until the objections to a realistic language are better formulated and justified, it seems that the best candidate for the ideal, or metaphysical, language is a realistic language. It is the only one of the three which can accommodate meaningfully all of the classical mathematics, which – as it will be remembered – was one of the interpretations of the criterion of adequacy. Appeals to ultimate intuitions, questionable economy, and dubious charges of artificiality and arbitrariness are hardly justifiable reasons for rejecting it. This is not to discourage, however, the development of conceptualistic and nominalistic languages for metaphysics. There is no way to tell precisely what can and cannot be done with a language until every possibility has been exhausted. Here we should follow Carnap's advice: "Let us be cautious in making assertions and critical in examining them, but tolerant in permitting linguistic forms." [56]

---

[52] Goodman and Quine, "Steps Toward a Constructive Nominalism", *Journal of Symbolic Logic.* XII (1947), p. 105.
[53] R. M. Martin, *Towards a Systematic Pragmatics* (Amsterdam, North Holland Publishing Company, 1959), p. 15.
[54] *Ibid.*, p. 15.
[55] Rudolf Carnap, *Meaning and Necessity* (Chicago, University of Chicago Press, 1958), p. 221.
[56] *Ibid.*, p. 221.

D. THE CHOICE OF A DESCRIPTIVE BASE

Having chosen a logical calculus and mathematical base which
is taken to be adequate, the next step is to choose its descriptive
base. In the preceding section only the problem of admitting or
not admitting class variables in the ideal language was discussed.
We must now raise the question of the individual variables – or
the primitive predicates of the language, for one determines the
other. The question is this: What are the basic concrete individuals which will form the basis of our system?

Two types of languages which are frequently discussed in applied logic immediately present themselves for consideration:
phenomenalistic and physicalistic languages. A phenomenalistic
language may take as basic individuals either momentary cross
sections of the total stream of experience, as Carnap's *Der
Logische Aufbau der Welt,* or phenomenal quale or sensa, as
Goodman's *The Structure of Appearance.* Such a language expresses the properties and relations between these phenomenal
entities. In contrast a physicalistic language has to do with the
properties and relations of physical things in a four-dimensional
space-time continuum. The basic concrete individuals in such a
language are usualy taken to be spatio-temporal slices of things,
or space-time regions or points of things. A thing is then defined
as a class of such slices, regions, or points.[57]

Despite Goodman's [58] reservations concerning a precise and
general distinction between these two types of languages, there
is certainly a difference between what is taken as the basic concrete entities of the language and, consequently, a difference between their primitive predicates and axioms. As he himself points
out, in speaking of phenomenal and physical space, "a change
of position in either may not be accompanied by a change of
position in the other".[59] Also, just as the choices between alter-

---

[57] There is an excellent classification and illustration of thing languages
in Rudolf Carnap, *Introduction to Symbolic Logic,* pp. 157ff.
[58] Goodman, *The Structure of Appearance,* p. 101.
[59] *Ibid.,* p. 105.

native logical calculi reflect basic differences in traditional philosophical positions, the same may be said for the choice between
a phenomenal and a physical language. A choice of a phenomenal
language, for example, reflects the position that nothing beyond
the phenomenal elements need be countenanced in order to explain everything, including whatever is meant by physical objects
in a four dimensional continuum. If one allows the individual
variables to range over sense data only, he reflects the position
of sensationism, etc. On the other hand, a physicalistic language
reflects the belief that nothing beyond the physical need be
countenanced in order to explain everything. Such a language may
be considered a modern explication of materialism.

There is no doubt that there is some value and a common-
sense core of truth in each of these two languages. And Goodman
may be right: they "do not themselves necessarily conflict, but
may be regarded as answering different problems".[60] When we
are faced, however, with the problem of one metaphysical language in which we can talk about every area of experience, each
has certain inadequacies – at least, in so far as they have been
developed. Whatever the virtues of a phenomenalistic language
may be, it must, if it is to qualify as the ideal language, be able to
include statements about what we call "physical entities". For in
talking about our world, we talk about things in a four dimensional space-time continuum and very seldom, unless we are
philosophers, about sensa. On the other hand, whatever virtues
a physicalistic system may have, if it is to qualify for the ideal
language it must be able to include phenomenal statements, for
everything which can be known about the world must eventually
be explicable in terms of immediate experience.

This problem of immediate experience has led the phenomenalist to argue for the epistemological priority of his language.
To quote Goodman, "to the phenomenalist, what cannot be explained in terms of phenomena is unknowable, and words purporting to refer to it are vacuous".[61] And this must include

[60]   *Ibid.*, p. 102.
[61]   *Ibid.*, p. 102.

whatever the physicalist means by things in a four dimensional continuum. But it is precisely at this point that the phenomenalist encounters his difficulties, and these difficulties appear, at present, insurmountable. The difficulties of defining a physical thing in terms of sensa has led some phenomenalists to reject a phenomenalistic basis as essentially inadequate. A good example of this is Carnap. In his *Der Logische Aufbau der Welt* he attempted a universal language based on a phenomenalistic base and found it inadequate. This failure led him later to argue that such a basis is essentially inadequate for explaining objective and intersubjective fact.[62] He was forced to a physicalistic system as the only adequate basis for a universal language.

The phenomenalist, of course, may retort, as Goodman does: "the physicalist has so far come nowhere near substantiating either the claim that phenomenalistic bases are inadequate for a universal language or the claim that some physicalistic basis is adequate".[63] And, in a sense, he is right. The simple fact that phenomenalistic languages have, so far, failed to give a reconstruction of the physical world in no way proves that it is, in principle, impossible. Likewise, all physicalistic systems which have so far been constructed have their own inadequacies, if they are taken to be universal languages. They simply cannot account for phenomenal entities. If 'green', for example, were to appear in a physicalistic language, it could, by the rules of the game, only be predicated of physical entities in a four dimensional continuum. And, as Bergmann has insisted, "sense data are more than philosophical moonshine".[64] They must be accounted for.

This dispute, which at present appears to be insoluble, has led some to advocate taking both phenomenal and physical entities as values for the individual variables and, since one cannot be defined in terms of the other, to take both type predicates as

[62] Rudolf Carnap, "Die physikalische Sprache als Universalsprache der Wissenschaft", *Erkenntnis*, II (1931), pp. 432-465.
[63] Goodman, *The Structure of Appearance*, p. 103.
[64] Bergmann, p. 137.

primitive. Quine,[65] for example, suggests "positing" physical entities as values for the individual variables. This, however, also leads to difficulties. By his own ontological criterion, which we have accepted, to be is to be the value of a variable. Thus he would be saying that the statements 'There are classes', 'There are phenomenal entities', and 'There are physical things' are all true statements, but extra-systematically would he be saying that the last statement is really not true, for such entities are only posited? Not only is this a rather unhappy solution, it is precisely what he would not let us do with reference to classes.

Bergmann[66] is more straightforward in his solution; he would accept both types of entities and both types of predicates as primitive. This, however, is essentially a Cartesian dualism which, as was pointed out above, is a violation of our criterion of coherence. It is an illustration of arbitrary disconnection. It seems that the wisest course to follow would be to abstract the common-sense core of truth from both these systems and see if they cannot be combined in one language without violating the criterion of coherence. Such a language, with reference to this dispute, may be called a "neutral language".

Although no one has developed a neutral language, it would seem possible to construct a language in which basic individuals of the system are taken neither as phenomenal individuals nor as physical individuals. On the contrary, they may be considered as extended individuals exemplifying both phenomenal and physical extensive relations, which may be defined in terms of a more primitive relation such as 'connected with'. This seems to be the program suggested by Whitehead in his theory of extensive abstraction developed in Part IV of *Process and Reality*.[67] If one includes in his linguistic framework a theory of classes or sets, then space-time points, the phenomenal and physical space-time orders, as well as geometric elements may be defined along the lines suggested by Whitehead in his theory of extensive abstrac-

[65] Quine, *From a Logical Point of View*, p. 17.
[66] Bergmann, p. 55.
[67] Whitehead, *Process and Reality*, pp. 449ff.

tion. In addition to the phenomenal and physical extensive relations, one would perhaps need an additional phenomenal relation such as 'qualitatively similar to', in order to formulate a theory of qualitative abstraction along the same lines as the theory of extensive abstraction.[68] This should furnish the necessary machinery for defining qualities, or quality classes, qualitative orders and aesthetic patterns. Whether or not one could define the extensive relations and the qualitative relations in terms of a more primitive relation would be an interesting problem in logical construction and economy, as well as assure the coherence of the system.

It should be pointed out that the metaphysical task as outlined in this chapter is not in any sense radical or new in the history of philosophy. In Book IV of the *Metaphysics* (1003a-1005b), for example, Aristotle, in describing the metaphysical task, speaks of this task as including a study of the axioms of logic and mathematics, the question of substance in its primary sense, and an analysis of such pairs of terms as 'one and many', 'part and whole', and 'similarity and dissimilarity'. The metaphysical task, as we have outlined it, is to construct a linguistic framework in terms of which we could describe the common world disclosed to us in experience. This included, as Aristotle suggested, the necessary axioms of logic and mathematics. The question of primary substance, at least as suggested in the *Categories*, that "which is neither present in a subject nor predicable of a subject" (1b), bears a close resemblance to the question which we raised: what are the basic individuals of the language? Class theory and set theory are attempts to explicate one aspect of the problem of the one and the many. And a theory of extension and qualitative similarity is an attempt to analyze the part-whole and similarity-dissimilarity relations. Certainly the task as outlined here is in the spirit of Book IV of the *Metaphysics* and the techniques of contemporary logical analysis and logical construc-

---

[68] For the suggestion of a formal theory of qualitative abstraction see B. L. Clarke, "Goodman on Quality Classes in the *Aufbau*", *The Southern Journal of Philosophy*, I (1963), pp. 15-19.

tion furnish us efficient tools for carrying out this task. If definite criteria can be agreed upon and if metaphysicians will take advantage of the tools which contemporary logic has put at their disposal, then metaphysics may once again recover its status as a science. Perhaps in the not too distant future Goodman's prophecy will become a reality:

... the day will come when philosophy can be discussed in terms of investigation rather than controversy, and philosophers, like scientists, be known by the topics they study rather than the view they hold.[69]

E.   METAPHYSICAL TRUTHS AND NECESSITY

Perhaps the most significant contribution which an approach to metaphysics along the lines presented in this chapter can make is to give an explication of 'necessarily true'. As was pointed out above, one of the key notions in Whitehead's definition of speculative philosophy is the word, 'necessary'. For it is what Whitehead calls 'necessary ideas' which distinguishes metaphysics from the empirical sciences. The statements of the particular empirical sciences are contingently true; the statements of metaphysics are necessarily true.

In Chapter III we made the distinction between contingently true, or a posteriori, statements and necessarily true, or a priori statements on the basis of whether or not we would allow an event or occurrence to falsify them, and the distinction between analytic and synthetic statements on the basis of whether or not their truth values can be determined by the logical axioms and semantical rules alone. Since a linguistic framework for metaphysics, as we have outlined it, includes extra-logical axioms, the statements which involve these axioms in their derivations cannot be classified as analytic. And it is precisely these theorems which are metaphysically interesting. These theorems and their extra-logical axioms would be classified as synthetic. If they are taken as neces-

[69]   Goodman, *The Structure of Appearance*, p. xiv.

sary, or a priori, then we are faced with the problem of synthetic-a priori statements. Thus we are forced to raise Kant's question: How are synthetic judgments a priori possible?

The first thing to note is that Kant's question is somewhat ambiguous. It may be a request for a description of the psychological process whereby one comes to formulate a necessary judgment, or it might be asking for the justification for calling a statement necessarily true. The first interpretation of the question makes the question a psychological one and the problem becomes a problem in psychology and need not concern us. The second interpretation of the question makes the question a logical one and, in this context, becomes: How does one justify the extra-logical axioms, and consequently the theorems, of a metaphysical linguistic framework as necessarily true?

In a supplement to *Meaning and Necessity,* Carnap introduces the notion of "meaning postulates" in order to expand the narrow notion of analyticity explicated here.[70] He suggests that the extra-logical axioms of a language are meaning postulates and, consequently, can be taken as analytic, if analyticity is taken in the common sense of "true by definition". At first this seems harmless enough, for the extra-logical axioms which express the properties of the primitive predicates are, in a sense, primitive definitions. And Carnap justifies this by pointing out that in choosing extra-logical axioms, or meaning postulates, logicians are "guided not by their beliefs concerning facts of the world but by their intensions with respect to the meaning, i.e., the ways of use of the descriptive constants".[71] Such a treament of the extra-logical axioms seems to recommend itself as a way of justifying our calling the theorems and axioms of a metaphysical linguistic framework, necessarily true. There are, however, two very serious questions that can be raised concerning this procedure.

One question has been raised by Martin.[72] How are we to distinguish a meaning postulate, or axiom, from any other non-

---

[70]   Rudolf Carnap, *Meaning and Necessity,* pp. 222ff.
[71]   *Ibid.,* p. 225.
[72]   Martin, *The Notion of Analytic Truth,* p. 87.

logical postulate or empirical hypothesis? In a formalized language for physics, for example, what is to keep one from taking a physical law or empirical observation as a meaning postulate? In the light of this notion of analyticity, it is conceivable that a language can be constructed in which any factual statement could be taken as a meaning postulate by arbitrary fiat of the logician and be considered analytic and necessary. There are no criteria to limit him, and without some criterion the notion of analytic becomes trivial.

The second reason for questioning Carnap's procedure arises from a problem pointed to by J. G. Kemeny [73] and Yehoshua Bar-Hillel,[74] and it concerns the restrictive nature of extra-logical axioms. This problem can be explained in terms of Carnap's notion of state descriptions. If we take, for example, a two place predicate such as 'warmer', symbolize it with 'W' and characterize it with an axiom as transitive, irreflexive and assymmetric, then the statements, 'Wab . Wbc . ~ Wac,' 'Wab . Wba' and 'Waa' are analytically or necessarily false in some state descriptions. Thus the possible true state descriptions are restricted by the meaning postulate, or axiom, which characterizes this two place predicate. This, in effect, limits the interpretation of the language. For this reason, analyticity thus broadened by Carnap is no longer a concept of pure semantics.

Both of these questions raised with reference to Carnap's treatment of analyticity point to the fact that the extra-logical axioms have to do with limiting the application of the linguistic framework to a particular domain, and consequently the problem lies outside the domain of pure semantics. For the function of extra-logical axioms, as Kemeny and Bar-Hillel have pointed out, is, in effect, to limit the interpretation of the language to a domain with a particular structure. And Martin's question raises the problem of how limited shall the domain be. Thus, it seems that

[73]   J. G. Kemeny, "Review of the Logical Foundations of Probability", *Journal of Symbolic Logic*, XVI (1951), pp. 205-207.
[74]   Yehoshua Bar-Hillel, "A Note on State Descriptions", *Philosophical Studies*, II (1951), pp. 72-75.

metaphysics is not only possible, but necessary for an explication of the distinction between necessarily true and contingently true statements. If contingent statements are those statements which some occurrence in, or some observation of, the common world disclosed to us in experience can falsify, then it certainly seems that the extra-logical axioms which limit the domain of discourse and characterize what we mean by 'the common world disclosed to us in experience' can justifiably be called necessarily true. However, to answer Martin's question, no statement which some occurrence in, or observation of, the common world disclosed to us in experience could falsify can qualify as an axiom in the metaphysical linguistic framework. Such a theory of necessity does justice to the common notion that a metaphysical truth is "true of all possible worlds".

VII

SOME APPLICATIONS OF SYMBOLIC LOGIC TO
NATURAL THEOLOGY

It is frequently conceded that natural theology was dealt a mortal blow by the *Critique of Pure Reason* and the *Dialogues Concerning Natural Religion*. While Kant is said to have exposed natural theology as a "dialectical illusion" and delegated the problem of God to the realm of practical reason; Philo, in the *Dialogues*, reduced natural theology to "one simple, . . . somewhat ambiguous, . . . undefined proposition" and suggested that "a person seasoned with a just sense of the imperfections of natural reason, will fly to revealed truth with the greatest avidity".[1] As we noted earlier, many of the philosophical offspring of these two men have gone a step beyond their progenitors and declared statements concerning God to be "meaningless", "ungrammatical", "expressions of emotions" or "blicks about the world". This study has been an attempt to suggest, with the help of the modern techniques of symbolic logic, an alternative to this tradition. In Chapter IV we suggested the possibility of formulating a definite description for God in terms of the primitive predicates of a linguistic framework adequate for describing the common world disclosed to us in experience and proving that his existence necessarily follows from the axioms and rules of this linguistic framework. In the light of our explication of the term, 'God', in Chapter V, we shall attempt in this chapter this task of natural theology in terms of one of the possible metaphysical frameworks discussed in Chapter VI. In order, however, to distinguish the program of natural theology outlined in this discussion from another application of logical analysis to natural theology, let us examine first the work of Jan Salamucha.[2]

[1] David Hume, *Dialogues Concerning Natural Religion*, p. 94.
[2] Jan Salamucha, "Dovód 'ex motu' na Istienie Boga (Analiza Logiczna

A. THE WORK OF SALAMUCHA

Salamucha's program is simply to analyze the proof of God from motion as presented by St. Thomas in the *Summa Contra Gentiles*, determine the presuppositions, formalize them, and give a rigorous demonstration that the conclusion follows from the premises. In his formalization he accepts the relevant logical parts of *Principia Mathematica* as his logical calculus. This is supplemented with the following non-logical constants: [3] 'B', 'R', 'M', 'A', 'P', 'S', 'F', and 't' with the appropriate subscripts. These constants are extra-systematically interpreted as follows:

DS1   'Bx' for 'x is in motion'

DS2   'xRy' for 'x makes y move'

DS3   'xMy' for 'x is a proper part of y'

DS4   'xAz,y' for 'x is in act under a certain aspect, z, with respect to y'

DS5   'xPz,y' for 'x is in potency under a certain aspect, z, with respect to y'

DS6   'xAr,y' for 'x is in act in respect to a certain movement, r, with respect to y'

DS7   'xPr,y' for 'x is in potency in respect to a certain movement, r, in respect to y'

DS8   'xBt_2' for 'x is in motion during time 2'

DS9   'Sx' for 'x is a body'

DS10 'Ft_2' for 'time 2 is finite'

The proposition which St. Thomas seeks to prove is, according

Argumentacji Sw. Thomasza z Akwinu)", *Collectanea Theologica*, XV (1934), pp. 53-92. This article has been translated and summarized in William Bryar, *St. Thomas and the Existence of God* (Chicago, Henry Regnery Company, 1951), pp. 211-219.
[3]   I have changed some of Salamucha's Greek notations for convenience. In the following definitions, 'DS' means 'definition of Salamucha'.

to Salamucha, "There is one and only one thing such that it is not in motion and it makes everything else move." [4] This he formalizes as follows:

$$(\exists v)(\sim Bv \cdot (w)((w \in C'R \cdot w \neq v) \supset vRw)).$$

St. Thomas begins his over-all proof with a brief proof which rests on two basic propositions, 'whatever is in motion is moved by another' and 'it is not possible to proceed to infinity in movers and things moved'. The first of these is formalized by Salamucha in this way:

S1 $(x)(Bx \supset (\exists t) tRx).$

For the second informal proposition Salamucha proposes the following two formal propositions:

S2 $(x)(y)(z)((xRy \cdot yRz) \supset xRz).$

In other words, 'R' is a transitive relation.

S3 $(x)(y)((x \in C'R \cdot y \in C'R \cdot x \neq y) \supset (xRy \vee yRx)).$

The next basic step in St. Thomas' over-all proof is to offer three proofs for his first basic proposition. 'Whatever is in motion is moved by another'. Two of these proofs, the first and the third, are analyzed by Salamucha in order to determine the necessary presuppositions. The first contains three:

AS1.1 $(x)(Bx \supset (\exists a)(\exists b)(aMx \cdot bMx)).$ [5]
AS1.2 $(x)((\exists a)(\exists b)(aMx \cdot bMx \cdot ((\sim Ba \cdot Bb) \vee (\sim Ba \supset \sim Bb))) \supset xRx).$
AS1.3 $(x)(y)(xRy \supset By).$

The third proof for the first basic proposition, S1, contains four presuppositions:

---

[4]   For a criticism of this interpretation see I. M. Bochenski, Review of Jan Salamucha's *Dovód 'ex motu' na Istienie Boga*, in *Bulletin Thomiste*, IV (1935), pp. 598-603.

[5]   The numbering is Salamucha's. 'AS' means 'axiom of Salamucha'. I have substituted the above notation for the *P.M.* notation of Salamucha.

AS2.1 $(x)(y)(z)(xAz,y \supset \sim xPz,y).$
AS2.2 $(x)(y)((Bx \cdot yRx) \supset xPr,y).$
AS2.3 $(x)(y)((Bt_2,x \cdot yRx) \supset yAr,x).$
AS2.4 $(x)(y)(xRy \supset By).$

Salamucha has only formalized, and then only partially, the first of the three proofs for the second basic proposition, 'it is not possible to proceed to infinity in movers and things moved'. This proof rests on seven presuppositions:

AS3.1 $(x)(Bx \supset Sx).$
AS3.2 $(x)((Sx \cdot Bx) \supset (\exists t_1)(Bt_1,x)).$
AS3.3 $(x)(Sx \supset (t_2)(Bt_2,x \supset Ft_2)).$
AS3.4 $(x)(y)(t_1)(t_2)((xRy \cdot Bt_1,x \cdot Bt_2,y) \supset t_1 = t_2).$
AS3.5 $(x)(\exists t)(tRx \supset Bx).$

To these five formal axioms, Salamucha adds two informal axioms:

AS3.5   An infinite body – and even a finite group of bodies which form *per continuationem* or *per contiguationem* one body – cannot move in a finite segment of time.
AS3.7   Bodies cannot act at a distance.

Either the first set of axioms, AS1.1–AS1.4, or the second set, AS2.1–AS1.4, plus the third set, AS3.1–AS3.7, are sufficient to prove the existence of a universal unmoved mover. The actual proof, based on these axioms, is not important for our purposes here. As we stated in Chapter VI, few metaphysical systems have suffered from being illogical. What is metaphysically interesting in Salamucha's work is the fact that such an investigation makes clear the necessary presuppositions, both the primitive terms and axioms, upon which the proof rests. This, along with the rigorous demonstration is all, however, that this method accomplishes. The question of the justification of the extra-logical terms and axioms has yet to be faced.

In evaluating the work of Salamucha, however, one must be careful not to criticize him for not doing what he never intended to do. He is only concerned with demonstrating rigorously and analyzing one of St. Thomas' proofs; he is not attempting to construct a metaphysical language. And Bochenski is perhaps right when, in reviewing Salamucha's work, he writes: "The work of Salamucha constitutes a real advance in the knowledge of the examined text and throws much light on the method of the Angelic Doctor." [6] Once the arguments have been analyzed, formalized, and proven valid, there is still the problem of the extra-logical terms and axioms. And, as we have stated, it is these which are metaphysically interesting for a theological language. In the closing paragraphs of his article, Bochenski points to this problem:

> The philosopher and theologian who wish to examine our proof have now all the material at their disposal: in order to see if the conclusion is valid, they must examine one by one all the eleven terms, carefully observing if they have a very determinate sense, and check the validity of the extra-logical axioms. [7]

Precisely what is involved here and how this is to be done, Bochenski does not tell us. If a complete logical analysis, such as the one presented here, could be made, for example, of all the philosophical section of the *Summa* and the various extra-logical terms and axioms determined, this would be the first step in constructing a Thomistic metaphysical language along the lines previously proposed. [8] The next step would be to see how many of the extra-logical terms could be defined in terms of others, thus reducing the number of primitive terms and systematizing

[6] I. M. Bochenski, "Review of Jan Salamucha's . . .", p. 601. (L'œuvre de M. S. constitue donc un progrès véritable dans la connaissance du texte examiné et projette beaucoup de lumière sur la méthode du Docteur Angelique.)
[7] I. M. Bochenski, *Nove Lezioni di Logica Simbolica*, p. 154. (Il filosofo e il teologo, che voglino esaminare il nostro testo, hanno ora tutti i materali a loro disposizione: per verdere se la conclusione vale, devono esaminare uno ad uno tutti gli 11 termini, badando se hanno tutti un senso ben determinato, e controllare il valore degli assiomi estra- logici.)
[8] Bochenski does mention that this is the ideal: ". . . un' analisi completa dal punto di vista logico rimane sempre l'ideale, qui come in tutti gli altri seltori della scienza", *Ibid.*, p. 155.

the work. In this way the language could be judged for its coherence and Bochenski's requirement that the terms have "a very determinate sense" be met. The next step would be an attempt to reduce the extra-logical axioms. This would result in the complete formalization of St. Thomas' system. Such a complete formalization of St. Thomas' system would give the philosopher a way of testing the system for applicability and adequacy, as outlined in Chapter VI. And it is primarily through these two criteria that the justification of the extra-logical axioms can be found. Let us turn now to one of the linguistic frameworks discussed in Chapter VI and see how the problem of natural theology may be treated in such a linguistic framework.

B.   THE LANGUAGE OF NELSON GOODMAN

In his book, *The Structure of Appearance,* Goodman takes phenomenal qualia as the basic primitive atomic individuals of the system, and his language is, according to the classification proposed in Chapter VI, phenomenalistic. And, since he does not include a theory of classes in his language, it may be considered nominalistic.[9] It is not the particular concern of this chapter to criticize the inadequacies of Goodman's system in terms of the four metaphysical criteria proposed in Chapter VI, but merely to illustrate how the theological problem can be treated in such a language. Some mention will be made of these inadequacies, however, in the closing section of the chapter.

The general apparatus of Goodman's system consists of the usual truth-functional signs, individual variables, the signs of quantification and punctuation, and a calculus of individuals based on the primitive predicate 'O', to be read as 'overlap'.

---

[9] There is some question of Goodman's nominalism. In *The Structure of Appearance* he is forced to revise his earlier position which was primarily eflected in the quotations in Chapter VI. Since he now includes "abstract individuals", he is forced to define nominalism as rejecting all "non-individuals" rather than as rejecting all "abstract entities".

Within the calculus of individuals there are three definitions which concern us here:

D2.041   'xZy' for '$\sim(x \bigcirc y)$.[10]

In the calculus any two individuals which overlap have at least one individual in common, and any two individuals which have no common content are said to be discrete from each other.

D2.042   'x < y' for '$(z)(z \bigcirc x \supset z \bigcirc y)$.
D2.043   'x ≪ y' for '$(x < y) \cdot \sim(y < x)$.

Thus an individual can be a part of itself, but not a proper part of itself.

The range of the individual variables is restricted so that only sums of one or more qualia are admitted as values. Qualia are taken to be such things as colors, times, visual-field places, and other non-visual qualia. These are the atomic individuals of the system. In addition to the primitive predicate, 'O', in the calculus, Goodman introduces a second primitive predicate, 'A', to be read as 'affiliated with'. In this applied calculus only the following definitions are important for our purposes:

DA-1   'Wx,y' for 'Ax,y $\cdot$ xZy'.

The predicate 'W' (with) applies "between two individuals if, and only if, they are discrete complexes comprised in a single concretum".[11] And by a concretum, Goodman means a fully concrete entity which has among its qualia at least one member of every category within some sense realm. Take, for example, a color quale located at a place in a visual-field at a particular time; this is a color quale *with* a complex composed of two qualia, a place and a time, and the three compose a concretum.

D7.01   'Qux' for '$(\exists y)\{Wx,y \cdot (z)(t)[Wz,t \supset \sim(z \ll x)]\}$'

---

[10]   The numbering system in this chapter follows Goodman. In my revisions and additions, I have followed his general plan. My own definitions and theorems are numbered D12.—— and 12.——.
[11]   Nelson Goodman, *The Structure of Appearance*, p. 173.

This definition of a quale defines it as atomic – that is, it can have no other quale as a proper part.

D7.03   'Cmx' for '(y)(z){[(y + z < x) · yZz] ⊃ Wy,z}'

Thus, a complex is defined as an individual whose parts, if discrete, are with each other. This definition, it should be noticed, allows all qualia to be complexes, but not all complexes to be qualia.

D7.04   '¢x' for 'Cmx · (y) ~ Wx,y'

A concretum, then, is defined as a complex which is *with* no other individual – that is, it is a fully concrete individual.

In the light of the three preceding definitions, one may distinguish qualia (Qu), complexes (Cm), and concreta (¢) in this way: Qualia are the atomic individuals of the system and have no proper parts. Complexes are those individuals which, if they have parts, have the relation 'W' holding between any two discrete parts. Concreta are those individuals which are *with* no other individual. If qualia are the atoms of the system, the concreta might be likened to the molecules of the system. In addition to these three types of individuals, Goodman also uses the predicate 'compound', which he does not define formally, for those individuals which are the sums of two or more concreta. If concreta may be distinguished from complexes by the fact that they are with no individual, then concreta may be distinguished from compounds by the fact that they, concreta, are complexes – that is, the relation 'W' holds between any two discrete parts. Concreta and compounds are the fully concrete individuals of the system, and since qualia and complexes, which are not concreta, are not fully concrete, they may be called the abstract individuals of the system.

Two other two-place predicates 'qualifies' and 'partially qualifies' which are important for our purposes are:

D7.05   'Kx,y' for 'x ≪ y · Cmy'
D7.06   'Kpx,y' for '(∃z)(z < y · Kx,z)'

It should be noticed that while the predicates 'A' and 'W' are external relations, the predicates 'K' and 'Kp' are internal relations – that is, whereas 'A' and 'W' apply between parts of a whole, 'K' and 'Kp' apply between the parts and their wholes. It should also be noticed that 'A' and 'W' are symmetrical, irreflexive, and non-transitive, while 'K' and 'Kp' are assymmetrical, irreflexive, and transitive. And in the light of these predicates, we may think of qualities as those complexes which are not concreta, but qualify concreta; and concreta are instances of qualification which are never qualities.

C. A FORMAL DEFINITE DESCRIPTION FOR GOD

In his chapter, "Of Time and Eternity", Goodman offers a very suggestive definition of the predicate 'eternal' and remarks: "Theologians have perhaps overlooked something here." [12] Taking this remark seriously, let us see what can be done with the theological problem in Goodman's system. The first aspect of God which was proposed in Chapter V was "the totality of all possibility, or possible predicates". In Goodman's language this would be the sum of all eternal individuals, the fully abstract entities. He defines an eternal individual in this way:

D11.06 'Etx' for '$(y)(Ty \supset xZy)$'[13]

An eternal individual, then, is an individual which is discrete from any time, and, consequently, it is not qualified by any time. It should be noticed, as Goodman points out, that "the eternality of an individual is no bar to its occurrence at some times and its failure to occur at others".[14] And wherever it occurs, it is identical with itself. It is interesting that in this definition, we have here defined, in what the author calls a nominalistic system,

---

[12] *Ibid.*, p. 286.
[13] Although Goodman does not number this definition (*ibid.*, p. 286), I have extended his general plan to cover it.
[14] *Ibid.*, p. 286.

ING LOGIC** 161

an individual which bears certain similarities to a Platonic form or a Whiteheadean eternal object.

In order to formulate a formal definite description of this first aspect of God, his abstract nature, we need a definition of the unique sum of all eternal individuals. Here we can make use of Goodman's schema for defining unique sums: $(\imath x)\{(y)(x \bigcirc y \equiv (\exists z)(\ldots z \cdot z \bigcirc y))\}$.[15] With this schema and the preceding definition of an eternal nidividual, we may characterize the Unique Eternal Individual, or the abstract nature of God in this way:

D12.01   'uei' for '$(\imath x)\{(y)(x \bigcirc y \equiv (\exists z)(Etz \cdot z \bigcirc y))\}$'

In order to characterize what has elsewhere been called the second, or concrete, aspect of God's nature, we need to characterize an individual which contains all that is temporal, or qualified by a time. First we can define a temporal individual as follows:

D12.02   'Tex' for '$(\exists t)(Tt \cdot Kt, x)$'

Here it is better to think in terms of a temporal individual rather than in terms of Goodman's concreta. Although all concreta are temporal individuals – that is, they are qualified by a time – not all temporal individuals are concreta – for example, a compound.

Again, using Goodman's schema for defining unique sums, we can characterize the unique sum of all temporal individuals, or the All Inclusive Individual, in this way:

D12.03   'aii' for '$(\imath x)\{(y)(x \bigcirc y \equiv (\exists z)(Tez \cdot z \bigcirc y))\}$'

As we have characterized them, the uei, like Whitehead's concept of the primordial nature, contains all eternal individuals, while the aii, like Whitehead's consequent nature of God, contains all temporal individuals. The uei, since it is not qualified by any time, is wholly abstract, and as Whitehead says of the primordial nature, it is "the absolute wealth of potentiality".[16] On the other hand, the aii, since it contains all temporal indi-

p. 47.
[16]   A. N. Whitehead, *Process and Reality*, p. 521.

viduals, is, as Whitehead says of the consequent nature, "the objectification of the world in God".[17]

Given these descriptions of the uei and the aii, it is simple to formulate a definite description for God in terms of the unique sum of these two individuals:

D12.04   'god' for '$(\iota x)\{(y)(x \bigcirc y \equiv (\exists z)((z=\text{uei} \vee z=\text{aii}) \cdot \cdot z \bigcirc y))\}$'

Thus we have a formal definite description of God constructed in Goodman's language, and one which is a formal translation of the informal explicatum given in Chapter V.

D. PROOF OF GOD'S EXISTENCE

Given the formal definite description for God, it remains to be shown that the existence of God, as characterized, necessarily follows from Goodman's linguistic framework. The first move in the proof is to prove that at least one quale exists:

1. $(\exists x)(\text{Qux} \cdot x < y)$ 7.1[18]
2. $(\exists x) \text{Qux} \cdot (\exists x) x < y$ 1, Q.T.
3. $(\exists x) \text{Qux}$ 2, P.L.

The next move is to prove that this quale is a time quale or it is not a time quale:

4. $(x)\{\text{Quz} \supset [(\text{Qux} \cdot \text{Tx}) \vee (\text{Qux} \cdot \sim \text{Tx})]\}$ Q.T.
5. $(\exists x)\text{Qux} \supset (\exists x)[(\text{Qux} \cdot \text{Tx}) \vee (\text{Qux} \cdot \sim \text{Tx})]$ 4, Q.T.
6. $(\exists x)[(\text{Qux} \cdot \text{Tx}) \vee (\text{Qux} \cdot \sim \text{Tx})]$ 5 and 3, P.L.
7. $(\exists x)(\text{Qux} \cdot \text{Tx}) \vee (\exists x)(\text{Qux} \cdot \sim \text{Tx})$ 6, Q.T.

The main portion of the proof is to demonstrate that either side of the disjunction on line 7 logically implies: $(\exists x)(x=\text{god})$.

---

[17]   *Ibid.*, **p.** 523.
[18]   In the following proofs the numbers (i.e. 7.1) refer to Goodman's theorems. A number with Q.T. or P.L. indicates that the step follows from the line so numbered by quantification theory or propositional logic. P.L. and Q.T. without a number indicates that the formula is a theorem of the propositional logic or quantification theory.

8. $(\exists x)(Qux \cdot Tx)$ hypothesis
9. $Qux \supset (\exists y)Wy,x$ 7.15
10. $Tx \supset Tx$ P.L.
11. $(Qux \cdot Tx) \supset (Tx \cdot (\exists y)Wy,x)$ 9 and 10, P.L.
12. $(x)[(Qux \cdot Tx) \supset (Tx \cdot (\exists y)Wy,x)]$ 11, Q.T.
13. $(\exists x)(Qux \cdot Tx) \supset (\exists x)(Tx \cdot (\exists y)Wy,x)$ 12, Q.T.
14. $(\exists x)(Tx \cdot (\exists y)Wy,x)$ 13 and 8, P.L.
15. $(\exists x)(Tx \cdot (\exists y)Wx,y)$ 14 and 7.27, Q.T.
16. $Wx,y \supset Kx,x+y$ 7.522
17. $z=x+y \supset (Kx,x+y \supset Kx,z)$ Q.T.
18. $(z)[z=x+y \supset (Kx,x+y \supset Kx,z)]$ 17, Q.T.
19. $(\exists z)(z=x+y) \supset (\exists z)(Kx,x+y \supset Kx,z)$ 18, Q.T.
20. $(\exists z)(z=x+y)$ 2.45
21. $(\exists z)(Kx,x+y \supset Kx,z)$ 19 and 20, P.L.
22. $Kx,x+y \supset (\exists z)Kx,z$ 21, Q.T.
23. $Wx,y \supset (\exists z)Kx,z$ 16 and 22, P.L.
24. $(Tx \cdot Wx,y) \supset (Tx \cdot (\exists z)Kx,z)$ 10 and 23, P.L.
25. $(x)(y)[(Tx \cdot Wx,y) \supset (Tx \cdot (\exists z)Kx,z)]$ 24, Q.T.
26. $(\exists x)(\exists y)(Tx \cdot Wx,y) \supset (\exists x)(\exists y)(Tx \cdot (\exists z)Kx,z)$ 25, Q.T.
27. $(\exists x)(\exists y)(Tx \cdot Wx,y)$ 15, Q.T.
28. $(\exists x)(\exists y)(Tx \cdot (\exists z)Kx,z)$ 26 and 27, P.L.
29. $(\exists x)(\exists z)(Tx \cdot Kx,z)$ 28, Q.T.
30. $(\exists z)Tez$ 29 and D12.01
31. $(\exists x)(x=(\iota y)\{(z)(y \bigcirc z \equiv (\exists w)(Tew \cdot w \bigcirc z))\})$ 30, R.S.[19]
32. $(\exists x)(x=aii)$ 31 and D12.03
33. $(\exists x)(x=(\iota y)\{(z)(y \bigcirc z \equiv (\exists w)((w=aii \vee\ w=uei) \cdot w \bigcirc z))\})$
                                                              32, R.S.
34. $(\exists x)(x=god)$ 33 and D12.04

Now we must show that the right hand side of the disjunction on line 7, likewise, implies: $(\exists x)(x=god)$.

35. $(\exists x)(Qux \cdot \sim Tx)$ hypothesis

---

[19] 'R.S.' stands for Goodman's rule for the existence of sums: "If any individual satisfies a given predicate, then there is an individual that is the sum of all individuals satisfying the predicate" (*Structure of Appearance*, p. 47).

36. $(\sim Tx \cdot Ty) \supset \sim(x = y)$ Q.T.
37. $(Qux \cdot Quy) \supset [(x = y) \vee xZy]$ 7.193
38. $[(Qux \cdot Tx) \cdot (Quy \cdot Ty)] \supset \{\sim(x = y) \cdot [(x = y) \vee xZy]\}$
                                                          36 and 37, P.L.
39. $\{\sim(x = y) \cdot [(x = y) \vee xZy]\} \supset xZy$ P.L.
40. $[(Qux \cdot \sim Tx) \cdot (Quy \cdot Ty)] \supset xZy$ 38 and 39, P.L.
41. $(Qux \cdot \sim Tx) \supset [(Quy \cdot Ty) \supset xZy]$ 40, P.L.
42. $Ty \supset (Quy \cdot y < (\imath x)\{Cgx \cdot (z)(\notin z \supset x \bigcirc z)\})$ 10 and Def. p. 284
43. $Ty \supset Quy$ 42, P.L.
44. $(Ty \supset Quy) \supset [(Quy \cdot Ty) \equiv Ty]$ P.L.
45. $(Quy \cdot Ty) \equiv Ty$ 44 and 43, P.L.
46. $(Qux \cdot \sim Tx) \supset (Ty \supset xZy)$ 41 and 45, P.L.
47. $(x)(y)[(Qux \cdot \sim Tx) \supset (Ty \supset xZy)]$ 46, Q.T.
48. $(x)[(Qux \cdot \sim Tx) \supset (y)(Ty \supset xZy)]$ 47, Q.T.
49. $(\exists x)(Qux \cdot \sim Tx) \supset (\exists x)(y)(Ty \supset xZy)$ 48, Q.T.
50. $(\exists x)(y)(Ty \supset xZy)$ 49 and 35, P.L.
51. $(\exists x)Etx$ 50 and D11.06
52. $(\exists x)(x = (\imath y)\{(z)(y \bigcirc z \equiv (\exists w)(Etw \cdot w \bigcirc z))\})$ 51 and R.S.
53. $(\exists x)(x = uei)$ 52 and D12.01
54. $(\exists x)(x = (\imath y)\{(z)(y \bigcirc z \equiv (\exists w)((w = aii \vee w = uei) \cdot w \bigcirc z))\})$
                                                          53 and R.S.
55. $(\exists x)(x = god)$ 54 and D12.04
56. $(\exists x)(x = god)$ 7; 8-34 and 35-55, P.L.

It should be noticed that in the preceding proof any existential statement would imply the statement '$(\exists x)(x = god)$.' This is precisely the requirement which we made on the statement of God's existence in our explication of 'God' in Chapter V. Also, since the statement asserting God's existence necessarily follows from the axioms of Goodman's language, then the statement is necessarily true with respect to the descriptive axioms.

E. AN EVALUATION

In order to make clear the value of the approach to natural theology advocated in this discussion, we need only ask the question: Having formulated a definite description for God and proven his existence in Goodman's linguistic framework, what have we done? First, we have given a formal linguistic framework for theological statements. This has very definite advantages. Natural theology need not be, as Philo put it, "one simple ... somewhat ambiguous ... undefined proposition". Not only does this offer the theologian a more precise tool for the investigation of his own problems, it is an answer to the critic who speaks of the "ungrammatical character" of theological statements. Such criticism is quite prominent in the book, *New Essays in Philosophical Theology*. Smart, for example, frequently uses such words as "senseless", "ungrammatical", and "non-significant" in criticizing statements concerning God.[20] Flew speaks of the "misuse of language" in reference to religious statements,[21] and McPherson tells us that "religious questions and answers are not capable of being expressed".[22] Such criticisms themselves are meaningless apart from some linguistic framework. The phrases "our language" and "ordinary ways of speaking" imply that there are certain specific rules for the use of a certain set of symbols, and rules imply that there is a framework. Unless the framework is specified, then the critic may be accused of poor philosophizing. In any case, when the theologian uses a framework, such as the one used in this chapter, then he can produce his rules and challenge the critic to produce his. The discussion can then be carried on at the level of linguistic frameworks.

The notion of evaluating formal linguistic frameworks was discussed in Chapter VI and criteria for choosing between them were proposed on the basis of a definition of metaphysics. If, of course, there are no criteria commonly agreed upon, there is no solution to the problem. In fact, one could even argue that there is no dispute. For the two parties of the apparent dispute are simply using different signs and different rules for different purposes. If, on the other hand, there are commonly accepted cri-

[20]   Antony Flew, ed., *New Essays in Philosophical Theology*, pp. 54, 55.
[21]   *Ibid.*, p. 166.
[22]   *Ibid.*, p. 138.

teria, then a very fruitful discussion of the various different linguistic frameworks can take place.

In evaluating Goodman's system according to the criteria of Chapter VI, there seems to be no problem concerning the coherence and logicality of the language. The way to meet the criterion of logicality, in regard to Goodman's language, would be to prove the system consistent. As yet, however, this cannot be done for his system is not completely formalized – that is, not all the axioms have been determined. But the chances are that there are no serious problems here. As for the criterion of coherence, this can be tested through an examination of Goodman's primitives. Since the range of the individual variables is limited to qualia and sums of qualia, we can take the one place predicate, 'quale', as basic. In addition there are two two-place predicates, 'O' and 'A'. Do these three primitives meet the criterion of coherence – that is, do these notions, in the system, "presuppose each other so that in isolation they are meaningless?" [23] Since the individuals of the calculus, based on the primitive, 'O', are limited to qualia and sums of qualia, then these two notions, 'O' and 'quale', are inseparable, and so far as the system is concerned, either without the other would be meaningless. The same may be said for 'A'. 'A' is applicable only to qualia and sums of qualia, and at the same time, there are no qualia which are not 'affiliated with' other qualia. Thus the notion of 'being affiliated with' and the notion of 'being a quale' systematically presuppose each other. Thus there seems to be no "arbitrary disconnection" between Goodman's primitives.

As a nominalistic and phenomenalistic language, however, Goodman's system suffers from the difficulties which were pointed out in Chapter VI. These are recognized by Goodman himself. As any nominalistic language, it faces the difficulties of including classical mathematics.[24] But, as Goodman points out, "the effort to carry out a constructive nominalism is still so young

[23] Whitehead, *Process and Reality*, p. 3.
[24] For Goodman's recognition of the problem, see: Goodman, *The Structure of Appearance*, pp. 35-41.

that no one can say exactly where the limits of translatability lie".[25] The other problem which Goodman's language faces is the problem which any phenomenalistic language faces, the problem of constructing the physical world upon a phenomenalistic basis.[26] This problem, like the problem of nominalism, needs further study. And here again we should perhaps listen to Goodman's cautious advice and "decide on its solubility after rather than before the problem has been more precisely formulated".[27]

In addition to an evaluation, or critique, of Goodman's linguistic framework as an adequate metaphysical language, there is also the problem of evaluating the adequacy of the formal definite description of God as formulated in the language. The informal explicatum presented in Chapter V characterized God in terms of his relation to any and every creature or event. When translated in terms of a metaphysical language as presented in Chapter VI, God will be characterized in terms of his relation to whatever entities the language takes as complete facts, or units of things real. A complete fact, in Goodman's phenomenal language, is a group of qualia associated together in a concretum. Our formal definition of God meets this requirement. Also, according to our explication of God, the statement asserting the existence of God, unlike the statements asserting the existence of any other particular facts, must be necessarily true. This condition has been met by our proof for the existence of God. $(\exists x)(x = god)$' is necessarily true with respect to the descriptive axioms of the language.

There are, however, certain questions that might be raised concerning the adequacy of this definite description. One may, for example, argue that all we have defined, using Goodman's notion of a sum, is an aggregate consisting of all concreta, rather than an individual unique being. Such an objection, however, obscures the subtlety of Goodman's language. In the first place, it should be pointed out that in Goodman's system God, as

---

[25] *Ibid.*, p. 40.
[26] For Goodman's recognition of the problem, see *Ibid.*, pp. 101-107, 301-306.
[27] *Ibid.*, p. 306.

characterized, is as much an individual being as any other concrete individual in the language; any individual is a sum of qualia.
Secondly, it should be noted that concreta are not discrete individuals and that a sum of concreta is not an aggregate of discrete individuals. Concreta overlap, have common parts, and are
internally related to other individuals – qualia. Even though the
denotation of the term 'God' is constantly changing, due to the
addition of concreta, and forming what might be thought of as
different states of God, these different states, likewise, overlap,
and each shares the common property of being all inclusive.

At this point one might well ask: Since the definite description
and proof of God formulated in this chapter is relative to Goodman's linguistic framework, is not its value solely dependent
upon the value of Goodman's system? Does not the problem of
the inadequacy of Goodman's language destroy the value of the
definite description and proof? In a sense, of course, this is true.
Any such demonstration is relative to the linguistic framework
in which it is formulated. Nevertheless, investigations such as
this have great value, independently of the question of the adequacy, or inadequacy, of the particular framework. The very fact
that the theological problem can be dealt with, even in this
limited fashion, in what proposes to be a nominalistic framework
– one that claims to make the very minimal ontological commitments – is quite significant. Also, a systematic investigation of
the possibilities of treating the theological problem in different
linguistic frameworks could lead to a determination of the minimum requirements of a language for natural theology. Perhaps
such investigations could lead to the conclusion that these minimum requirements are a necessary part of any language which
is a likely candidate for the metaphysical language. If so, these
investigations would prove extremely fruitful both to the metaphysician and natural theologian, and Whitehead's prediction in
the closing paragraphs of his essay, "Analysis of Meaning", will
become a reality. He writes:

When in the distant future the subject has expanded, so as to examine
patterns depending on connections other than those of space, number

and quantity – when this expansion has occurred, I suggest that Symbolic Logic ... will become the foundations of aesthetics. From this stage it will proceed to conquer ethics and theology. The circle will have made its full turn, and we shall be back to the logical attitude of the epoch of St. Thomas Aquinas.[28]

[28] A. N. Whitehead, *Science and Philosophy* (New York, The Wisdon Library, 1948), p. 140.

VIII

SOME CONCLUDING REMARKS

This study began with a quotation from the *Socratic*:

> ... philosophical developments ... have not only outdated arguments for the existence of God with modern intellectuals, but have thrown doubt on whether sentences mentioning God ever have any meaning.[1]

The purpose of the study has been to present an approach to the problem of language and natural theology, which, at the same time, takes advantage of many of the semiotic techniques which have been developed by contemporary philosophy.

In evaluating an approach to the problem of language and natural theology, there are two questions which must be asked: 1) Is this approach philosophically sound – that is, does it answer the challenge of the linguistic revolution? 2) Is it religiously adequate; does it violate the nature of religion as exemplified in the religious activities of mankind? In this particular context the first question becomes: Have we justified the possibility of meaningful metaphysical statements? And the second becomes: Can a definite description for God, formulated in such a language, furnish the language of revelation with an individual which can serve as the "living God who is active in the affairs of men?"

Both of these questions are crucial in contemporary thought. As for the first question, the philosophical question, it is common knowledge that the so-called philosophical revolution was generally taken to be the death knell of an already dying subject – metaphysics. In Chapter I, I quoted from a paper, "The Future of Philosophy", which Moritz Schlick read before the Seventeenth International Congress of Philosophy and which can be con-

---

[1] *The Socratic*, V.

sidered the first introduction of logical positivism to an international forum of philosophers. Of metaphysics Schlick said:

Most of the so-called metaphysical propositions are not propositions at all, but meaningless combinations of words; and the rest are not 'metalphysical' at all, they are simply concealed scientific statements the truth or falsehood of which can be ascertained by the ordinary methods of experience and observation.[2]

This insistence upon the semantical impossibility of metaphysical statements became one of the most dominant and persistent trends in the so-called philosophical revolution. Does the approach, outlined in this study, answer Schlick?

If we accept the contemporary tendency to treat descriptive meaning in terms of the syntactical, semantical and pragmatical rules of a descriptive language, then I think we have. Perhaps the most graphic way to see the value of the approach to metaphysics suggested in this work is to relate it to a section in Kraft's *The Vienna Circle*. In his discussion of the development of this broader criterion of meaning, Kraft points to the fact that now "the distinction, at first sight so obvious, between scientific knowledge and metaphysics collapses".[3] And so he concludes:

We cannot anymore dispose of metaphysical sentences by simply calling them meaningless. On the contrary, it must be conceded that one could even construct a semantic system in which metaphysical sentences are meaningful – a point which was always stressed by the Polish Logisticians.[4]

In an effort, however, to salvage the traditional position of the Vienna Circle concerning the questionable nature of metaphysical statements, he tells us that an empiricist will recognize a plurality of possible languages based on different syntactical and semantical rules, but he will recognize as "empirically meaningful" only those languages which meet two conditions. He writes:

---

[2] Moritz Schlick, "The Future of Philosophy", *Logical Positivism,* p. 112.
[3] Victor Kraft, *The Vienna Circle,* trans., Arthur Pap (New York, Philosophical Library, 1953), p. 40.
[4] *Ibid.,* pp. 40-41.

Now the fundamental postulates of empiricism select from all these languages a definite one: a language satisfying the requirements: 1) reducibility of the meanings of the descriptive signs to ostentation of that which signs designate, indeed of what is given in experience, 2) empirical testability of factual assertions.[5]

Not only has this study, I think, demonstrated the possibility of a set of semantical and syntactical rules for a metaphysical language, it has accepted both of Kraft's conditions. The first one is met by our criterion of applicability – that is, all the primitive descriptive predicates of the language must be exemplified in immediate experience, and all the other descriptive predicates are defined in terms of these. The second criterion is certainly acceptable. In fact, in defining metaphysics as we have, metaphysics, although not including any factual statements, delineates the class of factual assertions. Either the class of factual statements is clearly and explicitly delineated, or it is vaguely and implicitly delineated. And Bergmann is right: "An unexamined metaphysics, that is, one implicitly held, is for a philosopher the worst metaphysics of all." The approach outlined in this study not only offers a way in which a metaphysical position can be made explicit, it suggests criteria for judging the relative value of metaphysical positions and, I think, meets all the justifiable linguistic demands which contemporary philosophy can make.

There is, however, a significant question which should be raised concerning the theory of metaphysical, or necessary, statements proposed in this study. Granted that necessary statements are given a semantical interpretation and, in this sense, are neither meaningless nor non-assertive, is it not still true that they have no practical significance for human action? This question has been raised in a very pointed way by David Broiles. Concerning the position that 'God exists' is a necessarily true statement, he writes:

Let us grant that necessary statements do *assert* necessary states of affairs. And let us grant that 'God exists' is necessarily true. Then the statement 'God exists' is compatible with the occurrence of any

5   *Ibid.*, p. 41.

state of affairs. Then the statement 'God exists' is really like the statement 'it is either raining or it is not raining'. Both would be true and both are compatible with any state of affairs, for both deny nothing. But, and what seems equally important, while both may be assertive, both are *insignificant*. If, in reply to my question 'Should I take an umbrella to the game', my companion were to reply 'It is either going to rain or it is not going to rain', I should not feel obliged to thank him for this unimportant bit of information. I should not have my plans affected by such a reply, and would still not know what to do. If God's existence is compatible with any state of affairs, then that He exists is of little or no concern to mortals, for we shall have no cause to alter our plans in light of the truth of the necessary statement 'God exists'. In answer to the question 'How should I live my life?' I would find the reply, 'Well, there is a God, you know', of little significance if this statement were like 'it is either raining or it is not raining'.[6]

Richard Martin seems to uphold a similar position with reference to logically true statements. He writes: ". . . theorems of logic and the contradictions of such seem irrelevant to actions".[7] In order to treat this problem, let us take first the class of necessary statements which we have characterized as analytic – namely, those statements whose truth value can be determined solely on the basis of the semantical rules alone – and examine them. The statement, 'It is raining or it is not raining', would belong to this class.

Martin,[8] himself, defines the expression, 'X accepts the tilde in its normal sense relative to a language F at time t' in this way: '(a) if a is a sentence of F and tilde a is a sentence of F, then X accepts a at t, if and only if, it is not the case that X accepts tilde a at t.' The expression, 'X accepts the wedge in its normal interpretation at time t' is defined analogously. This means then that one accepts a logically true statement of a language F as true, if and only if, he accepts the semantical rules of F. But to accept the semantical rules of a language is to use those rules in investigating and describing the particular subject matter com-

---

[6] David Broiles, " 'Is There A God?' ", *Sophia*, IV (1965), pp. 6-7.
[7] Richard Martin, *Toward a Systematic Pragmatics,* p. 73.
[8] *Ibid.*, p. 40.

posing the domain of that language. Thus even the acceptance of an analytic statement does have practical significance for our behavior, since investigating and describing is a type of behavior.

In the same way we can characterize the acceptance of any theorem in a linguistic framework. To accept a theorem in a linguistic framework is to accept the syntactical and semantical rules of that framework in investigating the subject matter characterized by the non-logical axioms of that framework. It is precisely this fact that has led many, such as Findlay, to maintain that "necessity in propositions merely reflects our use of words, the arbitrary conventions of our language".[9] But it is the word 'merely' which is misleading, for the very use of the semantical rules in question gives an interpretation to the symbols of the theorem, and, consequently, the theorem is a statement about something other than the use of the symbols.

If we accept the theory of metaphysical, or necessary, statements as proposed in this study, then we can easily characterize the practical significance of accepting these statements as true. If, as we proposed, the non-logical axioms of a metaphysical linguistic framework characterize what we mean by the common world disclosed to us in experience, then to accept a necessary statement as true is to use the syntactical and semantical rules of that framework in investigating and describing the common world disclosed to us in experience. If, for example, we take Goodman's language as an example of a metaphysical linguistic framework, then to accept the statement, '$(\exists x)\ (x = god)$', as necessarily true is to use his syntactical and semantical rules in the investigation and description of the subject matter characterized by his non-logical axioms.

There is a sense, however, in which Broiles is quite correct when he tells us: "In answer to the question 'How should I live my life?' I would find the reply 'Well, there is a God, you know' of little significance." For the practical significance of the question of the existence or non-existence of God in natural theology involves only the question of methodology and what we take to

⁹ Antony Flew and Alasdair MacIntyre, editors, *New Essays in Philosophical Theology*, p. 54.

be the common world disclosed to us in experience – beyond that it does not answer the question 'How should I live my life?' In fact, a necessary truth by its very nature is no more relevant to one event than it is to another. This can easily be illustrated with the divine attributes which are generally taken as lying within the domain of natural theology. Take, for example, the attribute of omnipresence. To say that God is present in any and every event, makes his presence no more relevant to one event than it does to another. Or take omniscience; to say that God includes any and every event in his divine knowledge makes God's knowledge no more significant to one event than it does to another. Even to say that God includes all possible and actual value does not tell us that one thing might contribute more value to God than another thing.

This problem concerning the significance of God for answering Broiles' question – "How shall I live my life?" – points then to the second question of evaluation raised earlier: Can a definite description for God, formulated in such a metaphysical linguistic framework, furnish the language of revelation with an individual which can serve as the "living God who is active in the affairs of men?" It is, perhaps, this poverty, or religious emptiness, inherent in a definite description of God formulated in metaphysics which has led man, such as Pascal, to claim that the God of the philosophers is not the God of Abraham, Isaac and Jacob. At any rate, this claim of Pascal's echoes through much of contemporary theology. How much of this rejection of natural theology is due to a conviction that natural theology is religiously useless and how much is due to a conviction that it is impossible is difficult to determine. But it is a fact that since the devastating work of Hume and Kant theology has been making a steady retreat away from the entire problem of natural theology. Consequently, the problem of the relationship of the God of the philosophers to the God of Abraham, Isaac and Jacob is a crucial one in any contemporary study of natural theology.

In this study is has been maintained that in the religious tradition at least some sentences using the word 'God' have been taken as descriptive sentences, that is, as asserting something to be the case about an individual. It was also argued that the descriptive character of these sentences necessitated a definite description for the name 'God' and that such a definite description could be formulated only in a metaphysical framework, if the definite description was to meet the requirements of an individual adequate for religious worship. In effect, we have tried to argue that a natural theology is a necessary condition for religion as it has been exemplified in the Christian tradition. Now, however, we find that natural theology is not a sufficient condition for religion and that natural theology must be supplemented with revelation and revealed theology, if God is to be a "living God active in the affairs of men". And unless natural theology is so supplemented, the statements of natural theology may be interesting deducible theorems in a metaphysical framework but they would only have trivial significance for the affairs of men. Natural theology can only give us the most general aspects of God: his existence, his relations to any and every individual, or event, and those attributes which can be defined in terms of these relations. It can give us no more. Revelation is the means whereby men come to see God as uniquely manifested in events involving particular people and particular communities. It is through history that man discovers, defines and works out his destiny in relation to God and within the structure of the very general and universal relations expressed in natural theology. It is the function of the language of revelation to preserve these unique events so that they may have an efficacy beyond themselves. But as we maintained earlier, the language of revelation does not function merely as a description of events. It is not intended to record history, for the events depicted are taken, as St. Thomas suggests, as signifying something about God. But if this is the case, then that which is signified should be able to be expressed in a descriptive language; there must be a revealed theology. The *mythos* must be translatable into the *logos*. We suggested earlier the possibility of a translation of the revelation into statements about God's evaluations of the world, that is, seeing the revelatory events as his judgments, his 'yes and no'. Such an interpretation is certainly not foreign to the Bible, for it is precisely this idea of judgment which gives the Bible its dramatic continuity and it is through his 'yes and no' that he becomes "active in the affairs of men" or the God of Abraham, Isaac and Jacob.

The problem of translating the *mythos* into the *logos*, or the problem of hermaneutics, cannot be adequately treated until greater study has been given to the nature, structure and function of the language of revelation. It is certainly conceivable that through a study of the rules governing the language of poetry and drama, we may be able to formulate general rules of translation, or hermaneutical principles. A drama, for example, has a syntactical structure, but one which differs from the syntactical structure of a theory. There is a definite relationship between the sentences which compose it, but it is not the relationship of deducibility, rather it is that of dramatic continuity. Also, drama has a semantical dimension, as St. Thomas pointed out, but it is a far more complicated structure than the semantical structure of a theory. Here an analysis of the semantical structure of a metaphor may help in developing hermaneutical principles. Take, for example, the case in which fatherhood is predicated of God. One is saying that God's relationship to man is similar to a father's relationship to his son. Here the structure is far more complicated than simply predicating fatherhood of a man, for a metaphor signifies one relationship by way of another and struggles to give us what Ushenko calls "images which convey the impression of the 'living presence' of an object of description without forcing the imagination into counterfeiting the object by descriptive means." [10] Also, one must take into account the fact that the pragmatics of the language of revelation differ from the pragmatics of a theory. The signs used to preserve the revelatory events are intended to have an emotional impact upon the users which, as a matter of fact, theoretical language struggles to avoid. One of the main functions of the language of revelation is to

---

[10]   A. P. Ushenko, "Metaphor", *Thought*, XXX (1955), p. 422.

make the revelation efficacious beyond itself. Its function is not merely to describe an event but to make that event efficacious in the lives of men. As Brunner suggests, "it does not make me 'educated'; it does not enlarge my 'sphere', but it transforms *me myself*; it changes the one who receives it".

If these general syntactical, semantical and pragmatical dimensions of the language of revelation can be developed, and there appears to be no reason why they cannot, then rules of translation can be developed. In doing this the relationships between the language of revelation, the language of revealed theology and natural theology will become clearer. Perhaps then we will be able to see more clearly how the God of Abraham, Isaac and Jacob necessitates the God of the philosophers and how the God of the philosophers must be supplemented by the God of Abraham, Isaac and Jacob.

INDEX

analytic statements, 70-72, 149, 173
Anselm, 82-85, 90, 102
a priori-synthetic, 69-73, 148-151
Aquinas, 23, 72, 82, 86-89, 91-93, 96, 98, 100, 101, 108-113, 118, 119, 153-157, 169, 176, 177
Aristotle, 18, 19, 23, 72, 87, 99, 101, 113, 147
Augustine, 101, 116
Ayer, A. J., 15, 49f.n., 50, 60

Bar-Hillel, Y., 150
Bergmann, G., 51f.n., 128, 131, 133, 136, 137, 145, 146, 172
Blackstone, W., 27f.n., 43
Bochenski, I. M., 154f.n., 156, 157
Boole, G., 54
Braithwaite, R. B., 27, 28, 30-33, 35, 47
Broiles, D., 172, 173f.n., 174
Brouwer, L. E. J., 138
Brunner, E., 76-78, 115, 178

Carnap, R., 14, 49, 58-62, 71f.n., 73, 98, 142, 143, 145, 149, 150
Comte, A., 50, 52
conceptualism, 137, 138, 139-142
convictional language (see language, convictional)
cosmological argument, 45, 86-90

Dante, 23, 91, 93
Dawson, C., 75, 81
Descartes, 64-66, 72
descriptive language (see language, descriptive and syntax, semantics and pragmatics)

falsification criterion, 21, 63
Farrer, A., 74
Feigl, H., 49
Findlay, J. N., 24, 44, 47, 63-68, 174
Flew, A., 16, 21, 46, 63, 65, 165, 174f.n.
formalism, 138-142
Frege, G., 49, 52, 54

Garnett, A. C., 102, 105f.n.
Gilson, E., 103, 104, 114, 120
God, abstract nature, 106, 107, 116-118, 161, 162
—, attributes, 39-42, 90, 96, 100-103, 107-122, 175, 176
—, concrete nature, 106, 107, 116-118, 161, 162
—, existence, 13, 21, 22, 24, 44-46, 63, 81-90, 104, 120, 162-164, 167, 170, 172-175
—, knowledge, 108-118, 122, 175
—, meaning, 13, 27, 38-43, 84, 85, 88, 90, 98-122, 152, 160-162, 170
—, power, 118-121
Goodman, N., 73, 130, 133, 139f.n., 140, 141, 142f.n., 143-145, 148, 157-168, 174

Hampshire, S., 72
Hare, R. M., 20, 21
Harrison, F. R., 89
Hartshorne, C., 69, 82, 100, 101, 106f.n., 108, 114, 116, 118, 119, 121

JANUA LINGUARUM

STUDIA MEMORIAE NICOLAI VAN WIJK DEDICATA

Edited by C. H. van Schooneveld

SERIES MINOR

23. SAMUEL R. LEVIN: Linguistic Structures in Poetry. Second printing. 1964. 64 pp.   Gld. 8.—
24. ALPHONSE JUILLAND and JAMES MACRIS: The English Verb System. 1962. 81 pp.   Gld. 8.—
25. IVAN FONÁGY: Die Metaphern in der Phonetik: Ein Beitrag zur Entwicklungsgeschichte des wissenschaftlichen Denkens. 1963. 132 pp., 5 figs.   Gld. 14.—
26. H. MOL: Fundamentals of Phonetics, I: The Organ of Hearing. 1963. 70 pp., 28 figs.   Gld. 9.—
27. LÁSZLÓ ANTAL: Questions of Meaning. 1963. 95 pp.   Gld. 10.—
29. PUNYA SLOKA RAY: Language Standardization: Studies in Prescriptive Linguistics. 1963. 159 pp.   Gld. 16.—
30. PAUL L. GARVIN: On Linguistic Method: Selected Papers. 1964. 158 pp.   Gld. 14.—
31. LÁSZLÓ ANTAL: Content, Meaning, and Understanding. 1964. 63 pp.   Gld. 8.—
32. GEORGES MOUNIN: La machine à traduire: Histoire des problèmes linguistiques. 1964. 209 pp.   Gld. 22.—
33. ROBERT E. LONGACRE: Grammar Discovery Procedure: A Field Manual. 1964. 162 pp.   Gld. 9.—
34. WILLIAM S. COOPER: Set Theory and Syntactic Description. 1964. 52 pp.   Gld. 8.—
35. LUIS J. PRIETO: Principes de noologie: Fondements de la théorie fonctionnelle du signifié. Préface d'André Martinet. 1964. 130 pp., 36 figs.   Gld. 18.—
36. SEYMOUR CHATMAN: A Theory of Meter. 1965. 229 pp., many graphs, 2 plates.   Gld. 21.—
37. WAYNE TOSH: Syntactic Translation. 1965. 162 pp., 58 figs.
                                                                                  Gld. 21.—
38. NOAM CHOMSKY: Current Issues in Linguistic Theory. 1964. 119 pp.   Gld. 10.—
39. D. CRYSTAL and R. QUIRK: Systems of Prosodic and Paralinguistic Features in English. 1964. 94 pp., 16 plates.   Gld. 12.—
40. FERENC PAPP: Mathematical Linguistics in the Soviet Union. 1966. 165 pp.   Gld. 22.—
42. MILKA IVIĆ: Trends in Linguistics. Translated by Muriel Heppell. 1965. 260 pp.   Gld. 25.—
43. ISTVÁN FODOR: The Rate of Linguistic Change: Limits of the Application of Mathematical Methods in Linguistics. 1965. 85 pp., some figs.   Gld. 12.—
45. WARREN H. FAY: Temporal Sequence in the Perception of Speech. 126 pp., 29 figs.   Gld. 18.—
52. JEFFREY ELLIS: Towards a General Comparative Linguistics. 1966. 170 pp.   Gld. 20.—
54. RANDOLPH QUIRK and IAN SVARTVIK: Investigating Linguistic Acceptability. 1966. 118 pp., 14 figs., 4 tables.   Gld. 14.—